SPIRITUAL HERBALISM

The Beginner Herbalist's Companion: A Chakra-System Herbal Approach to Elevated Wellness with Plant Spirits and Nature's Most Powerful Curer

ASCENDING VIBRATIONS

Illustrated by
SEO RUQUE (INSTAGRAM: @SEORUQUE)

NOTE TO READER

The information in this book has been written strictly for general information and educational purposes only. It is not intended to serve as medical advice, to be any form of medical treatment, to diagnose any medical condition, or to replace the advice of a physician or medical practitioner. Please see your healthcare provider before beginning any new health program. Any use of the information in this book is the reader's sole responsibility.

CONTENTS

CLAIM YOUR BONUSES

To help you on your spiritual journey, we've created some free bonuses to help you clear energetic baggage that no longer serves you and manifest a life that suits you better. Bonuses include a companion video course that includes over 4.5 hours of empowering content, energy-tapping videos, powerful guided meditations, journals, and more.

You can get immediate access by going to the link below or scanning the QR code with your cell phone.

https://bonus.ascendingvibrations.net

Free Bonus #1: The 3-Step Chakra Tune-Up Course

Want to know a unique way to target the chakras? Elevate Your Existence by Targeting the Subconscious, the Physical, & the Spiritual

- Discover a unique 3-step chakra targeting method that so many people aren't taking advantage of!
- Hack your brain, elevate body, mind, and spirit, and release blocks holding you back from greatness
- Awaken amazing energy to tailor a reality that suits you better
- Stop wasting precious time on ineffective methods

Free Bonus #2: The Manifesting Secret Formula Toolkit

Are you done with settling in life, wasting precious time, and ready to attract your highest potential to you?

Free Bonus #3: The Spiritual Cleansing Toolkit

Are you ready to drop all of the negative energy that no longer serves you?

- Release energetic blocks that could be causing imbalances
- Awaken amazing energy to supercharge your aura
- Create a beautifully cleansed, energetic environment

Free Bonus #4: A Powerful 10-Minute Energy Healing Guided Meditation

All of these amazing bonuses are 100% free. You don't need to enter any details except for your email address.
To get instant access to your bonuses, go to

https://bonus.ascendingvibrations.net

INTRODUCTION

ARE YOU READY TO EMBARK ON A HEALING JOURNEY?

Hello, and welcome to the next phase of your life. If you're here, reading this, it's because you're meant to be. Something called you to pick up this book and begin to read. Chances are, it's because you desire a more in-depth knowledge of spiritual herbalism, but I'd like to believe that there is a more profound meaning as to why you've found your way here. This book spoke to you on a spiritual level and opened a connection that will begin a wonderful journey full of education and enlightenment.

I cannot begin to describe the absolute joy it brings me that you're reading these pages and ready to begin your spiritual herbalism journey.

This book is designed for the beginner herbalist with a deep spiritual intuition: An already deeply spiritual person who is looking to expand their relationship with the world around them. Whether you bring with you existing knowledge of the chakras, yoga, meditation, wildcrafting, herbal teas, and spiritual energies, or you're entirely new to these concepts, you will find everything here that you need to begin your healing journey.

I have taken a novel approach within these pages in order to make it simple for you to augment your current routine with new principles from spiritual herbalism. This chakra-organized approach will show you how to easily and practically energize your body, mind, and spirit using natural herbs. It will teach you how to use spiritual herbalism to target the chakras systematically, prevent over-stimulation, and keep them balanced. Because when your chakras are balanced, you are a happier, healthier, and elevated you.

Why design the book this way? I've noticed that many other herbalism books structure their chapters either by plant or by illness/complaint. This is fine if you are happy to read it from cover to cover and leave bookmarks at the parts you want to come back to, but it doesn't function most efficiently as a quick reference guide. This method also assumes that you have a physical problem you're trying to solve. Your chakras are responsible for your emotional, spiritual, and behavioral well-being, as well as your physical health. Many of the rituals you use in your daily life—meditation, yoga, essential oils, etc.— are aimed at keeping these energy centers in balance, not merely as treatments for when something goes wrong. The herbs and recipes in this book can be used the same way. Organizing the information by chakra allows you to quickly locate the information you need to balance your spiritual needs.

A BRIEF HISTORY OF HERBALISM AND HOLISM

Humans have been on this planet for tens of thousands of years, and for all of that time, they've had to deal with illnesses, injuries, and other health problems. Everything we know about human biology and medicine today is down to the discoveries that were made by our ancestors. Our modern understanding of medicine is influenced by a number of early medical systems created by different civilizations located all over the world.

One of the earliest medical texts ever discovered came from Egypt circa 1500 BCE. Called the Ebers Papyrus, these scrolls had over 700 recipes for medicines, salves, and other treatments, all using local plants. In China, plant medicines had been in use since around 2700 BCE, and in India, they were also being used in Ayurvedic treatments at a similar time.

We've got a lot to thank the Greeks and the Romans for because, as they made their way around Europe and Africa, they encountered a lot of different forms of herbalism and brought them all back home to be studied. The noted Greek physician Hippocrates wrote some highly detailed medical manuscripts in the 5th and 4th centuries BCE, compiling all the known information about the medicinal qualities of more than 300 plants and herbs. This included details about how to use willow bark to ease pain, an important discovery that is still relevant today because this is where the active ingredient in aspirin comes from.

HEALING THE SPIRIT

What is truly astounding about a number of these forms of traditional medicine is how similar their core beliefs are. Travel back thousands of years, and you'll find the ancient Egyptians, African tribes, Greeks, Chinese, British, Indians, and Native Americans, among others, all using the same (or equivalent variant) plant to treat the same complaints. Even the idea that there is an element to healing that goes beyond the physical—chakras, humors, energies—is present in numerous historical medical texts spanning different continents. This shows that the link between physical and spiritual health has been an important part of healthcare for thousands of years. Today we call this holism or taking a holistic approach.

Holistic medicine acknowledges that medicine should treat the whole person, not just the body. This should take into account their emotions, their mental state, and their physical well-being, as well as considering societal, ethnic, and familial influences. It is at the heart of traditional medicines like homeopathy, Ayurveda, Qigong, and acupuncture, as well as others that have died out or been replaced by more accurate scientific models. One such example is the teaching of Galen, which was popular all over Europe during the Middle Ages. Galen, an ancient

Roman physician, built on Hippocrates's research and envisioned the body being made up of four different humors (fluids within the body, such as bile and blood). Imbalances in the humors could be resolved by stimulating the opposite humor—a form of balancing act similar to the yin and yang of Chinese traditional medicine.

AYURVEDA

Still practiced all over the world today, Ayurvedic texts go back to the 2nd century BCE. These teachings look at the balance between the external elements in the universe—air, water, earth, fire, and ether—and the three internal energies called Doshas. Practitioners also believe the body is made up of seven tissues or Dhatus, each one responsible for a different part of the body's functions. Finally, Ayurveda considers the individual constitution of each person, called their prakriti, because this will determine how they react to different treatments and which ones are more appropriate. (Jaiswal & Williams, 2017). When something is out of balance, it can be corrected using herbal treatments, yoga, and meditation, with treatments prescribed depending on each patient's prakriti.

THE SEVEN CHAKRAS

The chakra system evolved parallel to the Ayurvedic Doshas. In fact, both have their roots in Hinduism. While the Doshas and Dhatus are physical systems, the chakras are wheels of pure energy, often leading people to refer to them as one's energy body rather than one's physical body. These wheels are constantly turning, allowing your life force to flow through your body, promoting physical and emotional well-being. You can draw links between them and the teachings of Ayurveda, and these two philosophies complement each other very well. Each chakra is influenced by a different element: fire, water, earth, air, ether, light, and cosmic energy.

Blocked chakras stop energy from flowing properly, and depending on which chakra is blocked, you will see this manifest as physical, emotional, mental, and even behavioral problems. Again, a combination of targeted yoga and meditation can help to unblock the chakras. They also respond well to certain colors, foods, and herbs, and you'll find more information on these later in this book.

You will find that the influences of your chakras often overlap with those above and below them. For example, the digestive system is influenced by the first, second, and third chakras, and this means that you might need to stimulate more than one to get to the root of the problem. It also means that many of the herbs listed in later chapters will affect multiple chakras and can be combined to create excellent tonics to revitalize your whole self.

ALTERNATIVE MEDICINE TODAY

Alternative and complementary medicinal systems have been around for much longer than modern pharmaceutical medicine, but they are no longer the main form of health-care. As a society, we now rely on doctors and pharmacists to prescribe treatments for a plethora of symptoms diagnosed in isolation. This is in direct contrast to traditional practices, such as Ayurveda, homeopathy, and Reiki, which seek to understand the causes behind our symptoms. These treatments look inward, investigating bodily energies and emotions, as well as considering the personality and spirit of the patient. Why else would the same problem manifest different symptoms in different people? Practitioners believe in taking a truly holistic approach, where the correct treatment would depend not only on the symptoms but also on the constitution of the person feeling them.

Herbalism is not a new fad; in fact, it is one of the oldest forms of medicine in the world. A lot of basic remedies that we use on a daily basis are rooted in thousands of years of herbalist traditions, even if we don't think of them as being based on herbalism. Things like using lemon-flavored lozenges or drinks to soothe a sore throat or rubbing dock leaves on a nettle sting. There are hundreds of others that would still have been common household knowledge as recently as the start of the 20th century. In fact, in less-developed communities around the world, herbalism is still practiced as the primary form of healthcare.

SYNTHESIZED PLANT EXTRACTS IN EVERYDAY DRUGS

Some alternative medicines have garnered bad reputations over the years due to misinformation and misunderstanding. What people don't realize is just how influential plants and herbs have been in every aspect of modern medicine. It is only since the latter half of the 19th century that our scientific capabilities have allowed us to create synthetic drugs, and even then, most of the chemical compounds labs produced originated from plants. These plant extracts form the basis for common drugs, including aspirin, morphine, and cough drops. Nowadays, 40% of pharmaceutical medicines use plant extracts or whole plant sources in their makeup (US Forest Service, n.d.).

Some of the newest medications in the fields of cancer care and dementia prevention are wholly derived from plants. For example, vinblastine is a chemotherapy drug used in the treatment of childhood leukemia and is manufactured from the dried leaves of the Madagascar periwinkle (Pavid, 2021). How incredible that an effective treatment for such a disease is entirely natural, and in order to make more, scientists have only to grow larger crops of this beautiful flower! Talking about plant-based medicine tends to conjure up images of herbal teas and homemade salves rather than licensed pharmaceuticals, but this is just further proof of the incredible healing power that plants bring if we use them correctly.

WHAT IS SPIRITUAL HERBALISM?

So, modern medicine agrees that plants are crucial to our health. Although many healing plant chemicals are now synthesized in laboratories, there have been notable instances, such as in anti-malaria medication, where these synthetic replications, despite being chemically identical to those produced by the plants themselves, do not have as beneficial an effect on patients (Rasoanaivo et al., 2011). Ask any spiritual herbalist, and they will tell you there is an obvious reason for this: you might be able to clone the parts of a plant, but you cannot replicate its spirit. And for spiritual herbalism, that's a pretty important part.

TWO TYPES OF HERBALISM

Within herbalism, there are two different approaches: allopathic and spiritual. Allopathic herbalism is most closely aligned with pharmaceutical medicine; it is designed to treat the symptoms and provide comfort and relief to the patient. In this approach, different plants are aligned with specific complaints; for example, peppermint will help with digestive issues, including bloating, cramps, and IBS symptoms. This does not take into account any information about the patient, other possibly related issues they may be experiencing, or their health as a whole. Allopathic medicine is entirely reductive: it sees parts, not a person.

Spiritual herbalism takes a more holistic approach. Spiritual herbalists encourage you to find the best plants and herbs to work for you. There are dozens of different herbs that have a calming effect on your digestion—not just peppermint—, and there are a whole host of reasons why some will be better for you than others. This is because spiritual herbalists acknowledge that plants have their own spirits too. Like people, there are some you are compatible with and others you are not. This relates back to Hippocrates and his idea of herbs—and people—having different qualities like dry, hot, moist, and cold. A cold person taking a cold herb will not feel better; instead, they should seek something hot and warming.

Although allopathic medicine can offer quick relief, it may simply end up masking the true problems. This is where spiritual herbalism has the potential to craft a greater sense of general well-being within its practitioners. According to Josh Williams, owner of Greenthread Apothecary and author of *Spiritual Herbalism* (2022, *p.197*), "It's about seeing the person as a whole, complex, and sovereign being who is more than just the symptoms they present. It's an invitation to explore how we feel and what we experience through the lens of our greater spiritual journey, and ultimately to truly heal."

IN PRAISE OF PLANT SPIRITS

Spirituality has been a part of healing medicine for thousands of years. Ancient cultures all over the world believed in gods and spirits that watched over us and could grant prayers and wishes. Mother Nature's spirits weaved their magic through plants, giving us access to thousands of healing and revitalizing herbs. A harmonious relationship between people and Mother Nature was vital for creating a happy and healthy balance. Nowhere was this more apparent than in Native American herbalism.

Native American herbalists understood that the healing powers of plants are gifts from Mother Nature and should be treated as such. Plants were picked with care so that the crops didn't suffer from overharvesting. They used as much of each plant as they could, always careful not to create waste. The Native Americans would even hold ceremonies and give tributes to the plant spirits, to thank them for their healing. This approach showed the utmost respect for every aspect of nature and cultivated a positive relationship between the Earth and the people living there (Kaulja, 2022).

A WORD ON WILDCRAFTING

Wildcrafting is the process of harvesting herbs that have grown of their own accord in public spaces. This could be in the wilderness—a state park, forest, meadow, or beach-side cliff—or in an urban location, like the side of the road or grassy verge. Foraging these uncultivated plants can be a wonderful source of fresh herbs, and many of those described in detail in this book can be found growing not too far from your home. You just have to know where to look.

Although wildcrafting sounds like a wonderful source of free medicine, there are some rules that one must follow:

- Take care not to wildcraft any herbs which might have come into contact with pesticides and pollutants. If in doubt, make sure you wash them thoroughly in a saltwater solution, as this will remove the majority of chemicals.
- When wildcrafting, remember that you are harvesting from a public space and never take more than 10% of the crop. Not only will this mean that other wildcrafters can find the herbs they need, but you are ensuring that the plants can seed themselves for the following season.
- Always ask the plants for permission before taking them, and remember to give thanks for their generosity. You will find that your herbs are more effective if treated with respect.
- Please refrain from wildcrafting in any way that damages the plants you leave behind. If you are cutting rhizomes, please make sure you leave enough of the parent root for the plant to survive. Please refrain from stripping bark from a living tree, as this will cause irreparable damage that the tree may not survive. However, if you go wildcrafting after a storm, you may find naturally felled trees and branches which you can harvest from.

HOW SPIRITUAL HERBALISM CAN ENERGIZE YOUR EXISTENCE

Modern life has changed our relationship with the world around us, and not always for the better. Nature is bulldozed to make way for endless houses, highways, and other human amenities. There are some areas of the cities where you can walk for blocks without seeing anything green and living. How can you tune in with nature if there is no nature to be found?

RECONNECTING WITH NATURE

Happily, there are simple steps we can take in order to restore our important relationship with Mother Nature. Cultivate your own green space; this could be a yard or balcony, or if you have no outside space, you can bring plants into your house or apartment. Inside plants increase the oxygen in your space as well as remove certain contaminants that reduce the air quality. But the biggest effects of having plants in your house are emotional and spiritual: they improve your mood, reduce stress levels, and lower your blood pressure (Royal Horticultural Society, n.d.).

If you struggle to bring nature into your home, you can always travel to the nearest park, arboretum, or forest space and fully immerse yourself in the plants growing there. Camping trips, even for the weekend, will give you plenty of time to commune with the plant spirits and start to reforge your connection with the natural world.

To start forming relationships with plant spirits, you need to use all your senses. Plants cannot communicate the same way that we do; they are much more subtle. Listen to the sounds of the plants rustling in the breeze, feel the texture of their leaves (gently!), and open yourself to feeling how their energy rhythms differ from yours. Spend time watching them, observing the subtle changes in their flowers as they respond to the weather and the seasons.

FINDING YOUR PLANT SOULMATE

I've already mentioned how spiritual herbalism takes a holistic approach, matching herbs to the whole person rather than prescribing based on symptoms alone. A trained herbalist, homeopath, Ayurvedic teacher, or practitioner of traditional Chinese medicine can help you find your perfect herb partner by analyzing your energy, constitution, and physical needs. However, Sajah Popham, author and founder of the School of Evolutionary Herbalism, suggests a more intuitive approach. Popham urges his students to open their minds and their senses to listen out for which plants are calling out to them. It might be that a particular plant keeps appearing in your life in different ways—random images, as a gift, an ingredient in several of your favorite foods, even literally appearing in your garden!—or maybe you have a plant that you are particularly attracted to and drawn towards. Stop outside a florist or in the park and see whether your eye is consistently drawn to a particular plant, species, or even just a color (Popham, 2016).

Another important consideration for spiritual herbalists is to look into your ancestry. We are a multicultural world now, and it is enlightening to learn from other cultures and traditions and see the different ways that people approach the same situation. However, a lot of spiritual power comes from your ancestors, your clan, and their ways of life which have been practiced and passed down for hundreds of years. This includes the use of certain herbs and plants which would have been found in one part of the world but not others. When looking for your plant soulmate, you may well find that the plants that appeal to you and work best for you are the plants you have an ancestral link with. So, if you're looking at a list of herbs with different native regions, rather than concentrating on which one is supposed to be most effective for your symptoms, consider the plan that most closely aligns with your own background.

FINDING SPACE IN YOUR LIFE TO BE SPIRITUAL

We all know how busy life can be: In fact, the speed at which modern life moves us plays a big part in the increasing number of stress-related issues and mental fatigue that people are dealing with. In between commuting to work, meetings, reports, managing the home, raising children, caring for loved ones, and the millions of other daily tasks we have to perform, it doesn't feel like there is a lot of space in life to slow down and nurture your spiritual side.

But, finding even a few minutes every day to check in

with your spiritual self and your energy body is vital if you want to stay happy and healthy. It's all about finding the right balance and giving yourself time to notice when things feel off before they lead to potential health problems. You already make space in your life for daily rituals such as brushing your teeth, reading the news, walking the dog, taking off your make-up, etc. Adding a couple of small, five-minute rituals into your day that tune into your spiritual needs should be all you need to allow that side of your life to flourish.

THE IMPORTANCE OF RITUALS

When I talk about rituals, I don't mean a lavish ceremony or any kind of sacrifice! A ritual is simply something that you do regularly and in the same way. If you always read the headlines while your morning coffee percolates, then that's your personal ritual. If you prefer to end your days by listening to your favorite podcast while rubbing lotion into your hands and feet, that's another personal ritual. You have intuitively crafted these unique rituals to serve your individual needs.

How you want to use herbs and plants in your daily routine is also entirely up to you. Everybody is different, so you must find the best way to incorporate nature on your own terms. There's no point telling you that you should start the day with a cup of dandelion tea if you don't like hot drinks. Instead, this book aims to arm you with the knowledge you need to make unique decisions about which herbs are going to serve your spiritual needs. To get you started with some ideas, there will be some suggested recipes and a guided meditation in every chapter. Then, in Chapter 9, you will find a 14-day plan with suggestions to help you integrate some of these wonderful herbs into your daily routine. The idea behind this plan is that it will give you a starting point to adapt and develop your own routine. You can substitute any or all of the herbs, recipes, and activities for others aligned with the same chakra.

THE ROOT CHAKRA

Your chakras stack along your spine, with the root chakra—also known as the Muladhara chakra—appearing at the base. Just like the roots of a plant anchor them into the earth, your root chakra is the grounding chakra. It is responsible for keeping you feeling balanced and in touch with reality.

ROOT CHAKRA ASSOCIATIONS

The root chakra also governs your basic instincts, such as your want to survive and need to feel part of a family. It also controls your desires linked to sleep, food, and sex. Basically, everything connected to your primal self comes from the root chakra. When this chakra is open and well-balanced, you will feel secure and confident that your needs will be met. It will provide you with an abundance of energy and a general love of life.

However, with such important behaviors associated with the root chakra, any disruption or blockage can have serious consequences. Many issues with the root chakra are caused by fear, for example, worrying about money, losing your job, or arguments in the family. These changes would all shake your sense of security, so it's no wonder they affect your grounding chakra.

Your root chakra doesn't just influence your energy body; it is also aligned with aspects of your physical body too. Your skeletal system and immune system are ruled by your root chakra. That makes sense when you consider that your bones are what holds you together and your immune system protects you—it's those basic needs again. Other body parts associated with the root chakra are your feet, legs, kidneys, adrenal glands, and lower digestive system (colon, bladder, and rectum).

WHAT INFLUENCES THE ROOT CHAKRA?

Each chakra not only dictates the energy flow through different parts of your body, but they also connect you to the wider world through external influences. Different elements, planets, colors, star signs, gems, and senses all share their powers with your chakras and help to determine their characteristics and how they can guide you.

(*Mars*)

The root chakra is influenced by the earth element. This brings stability and realism, helping you to connect with day-to-day life and feel secure in your surroundings. You can reconnect with your root chakra by spending time in nature and recharging from the earth. Walk around barefoot or sit on the ground to get the most benefit. This affinity with nature is echoed by the root chakra's pairing with the planet Mars. Mars also channels energy to bring you physical strength and the strength of convictions. It rules over your ability to make the right choices in life, something that can be affected if your root chakra is out of alignment.

(*The Waxing Moon*)

The root chakra is also influenced by the waxing moon. This is a time of positive change and immense new energy, and it can bring you new-found self-confidence. During the waxing moon, your connection to your root chakra is especially strong, so this is a great time to invest in its well-being and give it a supercharge. Take a day or two every cycle to focus on chakra-specific meditations, foods, and rituals using some of the herbs in this book in order to keep your sacred energy flowing smoothly.

Each chakra also has a ruling deity, and the ruling deity for the root chakra is the Hindu god Ganesha. Considered the supreme god by some Hindu sects, he is widely revered and worshiped by all followers of the religion. It is believed that he resides in everyone at the base of the spine, which would correlate to the root chakra. From this spot, Ganesha can support all the other chakras and rule over the energy body.

HOW TO KNOW IF YOUR ROOT CHAKRA NEEDS HELP

When your root chakra is blocked, your life energy cannot flow as effectively around your lower body. When the parts of your body that are under the influence of this chakra are deprived of this energy, they will stop functioning as normal.

Signs that your root chakra is out of balance include:

- Feeling angry, aggressive, and wanting to lash out at others.
- Worrying and obsessing over small details, trying to keep control, and becoming domineering.
- Losing your willpower or self-control, becoming unable to resist temptations, or struggling with difficult tasks.
- Feeling depressed, having low energy, and lacking focus.
- Feeling anxious, constantly nervous, and having trouble relaxing and switching off at the end of the day.
- When your root chakra is blocked, it can manifest as physical problems as well as emotional:
- Digestive issues are common, including constipation, cramps, and even a tendency towards eating disorders or binge eating.

- Issues with your adrenal glands, which can leave you feeling fatigued, both physically and emotionally.
- Pain around your lower back, legs, knees, ankles, and feet. A blocked root chakra can also lead to the worsening of arthritic conditions, as well as water retention and varicose veins in the legs.

USING HERBS TO UNBLOCK YOUR ROOT CHAKRA

Because your chakras exist as part of your energy body, not your physical body, they need to connect spiritually with anything you use to realign or unblock them. There are lots of herbs that are said to aid problems like digestive issues, joint pain, and fatigue, but they won't necessarily be the right herbs to work for you. The herbs listed in this chapter have been specially selected because of their natural and spiritual affinity with the root chakra. This connection is long established and comes from the wisdom of thousands of years of herbalist practices.

In general, the root chakra is stimulated by eating spicy foods, vegetables that have grown under the ground, and anything that shares its influential color: red. At the end of this chapter, you will find suggestions for some recipes that can be used to recharge your root chakra, but you can also take any of the influential herbs as an extract, tincture, decoction, or tea.

ROOT CHAKRA HEALING WITH NATURE

Your root chakra is the center of your earthy, grounded energy. It is the chakra that is most receptive to Mother Nature and the natural world, which makes it the perfect place to begin your herbalism healing journey. Here, I have outlined some of the most powerful herbs for unblocking and stimulating your root chakra. You should be able to find them in a good apothecary, food store, or even growing wild in your own backyard.

Dandelion (Taraxacum Officinale)

Dandelion is a fantastic herb that has been used for centuries in herbal medicine. There are records of its medicinal qualities as far back as the tenth century. It's a distinctive and cheerful plant found everywhere in the temperate Northern Hemisphere. Dandelion's jagged green leaves have a smooth, hairless texture and have been described as looking like a lion's teeth. Its flowers are yellowy orange with a spray of long, thin petals that form a hemispherical shape. Dandelion can easily be foraged from any grassy area, even in the city.

It grows prolifically and naturally as a weed and is highly self-propagating. When growing the plants, it is a good idea to remove the flower heads before they can seed themselves, or you will find your garden overrun! Flowers start to appear in early summer, but leaves and plants remain all year round. It's extremely hardy and will flower year after year if not picked.

The best part of the dandelion to use is the root, which can grow more than 12 in. long in good soil. The root should be dried before it is cut, as this stops the milky sap within from leaking out. This dried root can be made into a simple decoction or boiled into a tea. You can also use the leaf in salads, and the flower is used in England to make dandelion wine.

When using dandelion root in herbalism, you're mostly looking to extract taraxacin, a soluble, bitter-tasting sugar, and inulin, an insoluble, starchy prebiotic. Both are present in different quantities at different times of the year. Roots collected in autumn can contain up to 25% inulin, whereas roots collected in the spring are rich in taraxacin.

Dandelion is a cooling, drying herb and works well to counter complaints from people who have a hot or damp constitution. Dandelion root has historically been used as a diuretic and to treat a number of liver disorders. This versatile herb is ruled by Jupiter, indicating its link to the liver.

The leaf can work to improve kidney and urinary function. The root is commonly taken to help improve liver function, digestive health, and relieve constipation. You can use dandelion root to make tinctures, teas, and decoctions.

Anyone with an allergy to pollen should avoid dandelion, as it may cause a similar reaction. Because dandelion has diuretic properties, if you are taking other diuretic medicine, then you should consult with a doctor before taking dandelion as well. You should also check with your doctor before using dandelion if you have diabetes or gallbladder problems. Dandelion should not be taken by anyone on blood thinners.

GINGER (ZINGIBER OFFICINALE)

This useful herb doesn't grow in the wild outside of Asia but can be cultivated inside glasshouses or in fields where the conditions are similar to its native climate. This is why it grows so well in places like Jamaica, the West Indies, and Northern Africa, where it was transported in order to be grown in commercial plantations. The soil should be kept between 71 °F and 77 °F and must be at least 12 in. deep in order to get good root growth. Keep the soil moist, and don't allow it to dry out; otherwise, you will damage the plant.

If you're growing your ginger inside, you can grow and harvest your ginger all year round. Otherwise, you'll need to take it inside during colder months or at least make sure that the roots are well protected. Ginger is a type of rhizome; this means that the roots form branching systems, and you can harvest the outer branches without damaging the main structure. By doing this carefully, you can keep the plant alive and harvest from it again next season.

Ginger has been used for digestive health for thousands of years. You can find mention of this warming spice in writings by Confucius, Shakespeare, and Marco Polo, and it even pops up in the Koran. In Europe, during the Middle Ages, it was the second most popular spice for cooking and medicinal use (Banyan Botanicals, n.d.). Ginger is also well-known for helping with all types of nausea and is recommended to battle morning sickness and some of the side effects of chemotherapy treatments.

The ginger root is used in a number of different ways. You can buy the root dried or preserved in syrup, as a paste, or in powdered form. It is often added to dishes because of its warm, spicy flavor and is popular in everything from curries to cakes and even tea.

Some forms of flowering ginger plants have edible flowers, buds, and leaves. But unless you know which type you have, it's probably safest not to try them. The common ginger, where we get our roots from, does have edible flowers and leaves. They don't have as strong a flavor as the root, but they go nicely in salads or as a garnish.

Ginger is made up of more than 400 different compounds, but the one that helps your digestion is called gingerol. It speeds up the digestive process and stops food from hanging around in your gut for too long. It is one of the well-known herbs ruled by the moon. This alliance is known to benefit digestive health, which is where its influence over the colon helps to keep your root chakra open. Because of its spiciness, you might think ginger is a warming herb, but it actually has both warming and cooling properties. After an initial heating flush, it eventually cools and nourishes.

Ginger is a great universal herb with many benefits, but there are some people that should be careful about taking it in large quantities. Ginger can work as a blood thinner, so if you are already taking blood thinners or if you have a bleeding disorder, you should avoid ginger supplements if you have not spoken to your doctor first.

Ashwagandha (Withania Somnifera)

Ashwagandha is an important herb in Ayurvedic practice because it has so many wonderful qualities. It's native to a few regions, including India, the Middle East, and Northern Africa, but if you live in the northern temperate zone, you should be able to plant and grow it quite happily. Keep the soil well-drained; this herb is used to dry conditions and is capable of surviving through a season of drought, so you don't need to panic about under-watering it. It thrives in sunny areas with temperatures of between 70 °F and 95 °F. It is best to start planting in early spring because the plants can take several months to grow to maturity. This way, the roots will be ready to harvest in the autumn.

Other names for ashwagandha include winter cherry—because of its small red berries—and Indian ginseng—because, like ginseng, it can increase your energy levels. However, both of these names are a little misleading because it actually belongs to the nightshade plant family.

The plants can grow up to a meter tall and are completely covered in distinctive silver hairs. Before fruiting, you will see lovely star-shaped flowers in yellow and white. You can eat the ashwagandha berries, but they taste very bitter. The best parts of the plant to use are the leaves and the root. These are often sold as a powder, and you can make your own by drying out the harvested parts and then crushing them into a powder.

The easiest way to take ashwagandha root supplements is in the form of capsules, but you can also use the powder to make a tonic, brew as a tea, or add to another form of hot drink such as a latte or hot cocoa. It works well in hot drinks because it is a warming herb. Ashwagandha is ruled by the moon and the sun, with each celestial body contributing to a different side of its nature: The sun stimulates its rejuvenating qualities, while the moon influences its affinity with your emotions.

This versatile herb is useful in many different ways. It has traditionally been used as a sleep aid and for calming nervous conditions. It has adaptogenic qualities that have been proven to combat the effects of anxiety, stress, and fatigue. This is where ashwagandha's multifaceted nature shines: not only can it help you sleep better, but it also gives you more energy! This is a really intelligent plant because it always figures out the best way to help whoever has taken it.

Ashwagandha works with your root chakra by supporting your adrenal glands and helping them to work properly. It also targets your joints and your back, helping to keep your life force flowing smoothly through the lower parts of your body. Recent studies (Tharakan et al., 2021) have also proven ashwagandha to have the amazing ability to stimulate your immune system—no wonder it's known all over the world as the top rejuvenating and revitalizing herb!

If you have a hot constitution, you might want to consider taking ashwagandha alongside cooling herbs that will counteract its heating qualities. It is not recommended for use if you are pregnant because large doses can have a negative effect on your uterus. Large doses can also cause digestive discomfort, so if you have known issues in this area, consult with your doctor before taking ashwagandha supplements.

Turmeric (Curcuma Longa)

A staple in most kitchen cupboards, turmeric is used to add flavor to many spicy dishes. But it has other uses as well and can be taken as a supplement or used in larger quantities to help re-energize your root chakra. Turmeric is native to southern Asia, where there is a warm, wet, tropic climate. Although it is also a rhizome, like ashwagandha, it needs much more care to thrive; turmeric won't tolerate drying out, so it should be kept in hot, moist soil at all times. Outside its natural habitat, it is best grown inside.

When turmeric grows well, it can be almost one meter tall, with long rubbery green leaves, each growing from a single stem in the ground. This herb produces conical heads of small, yellow flowers in the late summer. However, the useful part of this plant is the root. Turmeric is part of the same plant family as ginger, and its rhizomes and roots look very similar. You can harvest the rhizomes by cutting off the outer fingers: this shouldn't kill the main plant and will mean you can have more to harvest the following season.

The main active ingredient in turmeric root is called curcumin. Many of the turmeric supplements you buy in the stores contain curcumin extract rather than using the whole root. However, by only using part of the root, you are missing out on many of the other beneficial actions of this herb. If you buy or grow your own turmeric roots, it's really easy to make a whole herb powder—just dry the roots out until they are brittle and then pop them in a food processor, blender, or coffee grinder! This will make a nourishing powder you can add to recipes for a wonderful boost to your root chakra.

Turmeric has always been used as an anti-inflammatory medicine, with particular influence over your body's joints. It also helps to support the immune system and your liver: these are all associated with your root chakra, so keeping these organs and systems in good condition will help your energy flow and keep your chakra open. Turmeric also helps you to maintain a healthy digestive system, and its warming influence helps to promote the production of new blood cells.

Like many other herbs with a hot constitution, turmeric is ruled by the sun. Its spicy taste and warming properties mean that it brings energy and rejuvenation with its healing. This is why it is seen as a stimulating herb. However, its anti-inflammatory qualities actually work by cooling the joints and calming the swelling tissue. Unlike ashwagandha, turmeric doesn't need to be taken with cooling herbs.

Turmeric is one of the safest herbs to take, especially when it is used in small quantities for cooking. If you want to take larger amounts as a supplement, you should check with your doctor if you have certain liver-related conditions, including jaundice, hepatitis, and gallstones. You should also avoid turmeric if you are taking blood thinners or medication to control your platelets.

RECIPES AND RELAXATION

Looking for some ways to perk up your root chakra? Why not try one of these recipes? You can always play around with them and adjust the flavor to your personal taste; just remember that adding chakra-specific herbs and vegetables will give you added benefits.

. . .

Red Berry Root Booster

Your root chakra can be re-energized and nourished through your diet. It responds particularly well to anything red, and this smoothie is loaded with red berry goodness. Proteins are also very beneficial for this chakra, so I've used almond milk, but you could use any other milk if that's not something you regularly buy.

You will need:

- 1 ripe banana
- 2 cups strawberries, fresh or frozen
- 1 cup raspberries
- 1 cup cherries
- 1 ½ cups almond milk

Add all the fruit to your juicer or blender, then pour the milk over the top. Blend until smooth. For a thinner smoothie, use less banana or remove altogether.

Warming Root Chakra Soup

This filling soup uses the root vegetables carrot and parsnip as its base, but you could also use sweet potato. The finished product should be smooth and flavorsome, and the spices will give it a lovely warm aroma. Ginger is great for targeting digestive issues, and turmeric targets and reduces inflammation, especially in the lower back and legs. This recipe makes two good-sized portions, so you can share with a friend or freeze some for another day.

You will need:

1 tbsp oil

- 3 medium carrots
- 1 medium parsnip
- ½ white onion
- 1" ginger, grated
- 1 tsp turmeric
- 1 clove of garlic
- 1/2l vegetable stock

Chop the carrots, parsnip, and onion, and then fry in the oil over medium heat for 10 minutes. Stir frequently to prevent the vegetables from sticking to the pan. Add the ginger, turmeric, and garlic and cook for five more minutes.

Add the hot vegetable stock and turn up the temperature so that the mixture boils. Then, leave it all to simmer for 15 minutes or until the carrots and parsnips have gone soft. Blend until smooth and serve with a coriander garnish.

For an extra boost, add some rosemary focaccia on the side.

You Can't "Beet" This Chakra Juice

Beetroot is one of the best foods for repairing your root chakra. Not only is it a root vegetable, so it brings wonderful grounding energy, but it is also a deep red: two benefits in one! It also helps to lower your blood pressure and is a really good antioxidant.

Lots of beet juice recipes tend to be savory, but this one is naturally sweetened by the watermelon—another red root chakra booster. The recipe below makes roughly one liter, so make sure you store extra in the refrigerator and drink within a couple of days.

You will need:

- 1 cup watermelon juice
- 1 cup coconut water
- 1 cup pineapple juice
- ½ cup beet juice
- ½ cup lime juice

- pink Himalayan salt to taste

Mix together and stir. For extra refreshment in the summer, blend the juice with some ice for a frosty slushy.

ROOT CHAKRA MEDITATION

Before beginning any meditation, you might want to prepare the room to make sure that it has a calming energy. Remove any clutter, turn down the lights, and ensure that you won't be interrupted. Your root chakra is associated with the sense of smell, so to enhance your experience, you can use essential oils, either in a diffuser, burner or as a spray. The best essential oils for stimulating your root chakra include patchouli, cedar, cinnamon, and myrrh. Another way to bring herbs into your meditation routine is to use bowls of potpourri to stimulate your senses. Choose red flowers to align with your root chakra and top up with drops of essential oils as the natural scent fades.

You might want to perform this meditation on the ground to get as close as possible to this chakra's element of earth. Settle into a comfortable position, either sitting or lying down, and close your eyes. Concentrate on the color red. Imagine red flowers growing up around you, their petals opening wide to the sun. Imagine putting down your own roots, just like these flowers. Feel the roots making your limbs heavier as they pull them down into the earth below.

As you take a breath in, imagine you are drawing energy from the earth along these roots. Feel the earth's energy collecting at the base of your spine. As you keep breathing, drawing more warming earth energy, imagine it filling your entire pelvis, spreading down your legs and to the ends of your toes. Give this energy the color red, and visualize your lower body slowly turning red as it draws the energy from the earth.

Finish your meditation by chanting the syllable *lam* on your final five exhalations. Slowly move your fingers, toes, arms, and legs. Finally, open your eyes.

2

THE SACRAL CHAKRA

Just above your root chakra is your sacral chakra or Svadhisthana chakra. It is found about 2in underneath your navel, and this placing is important because its location is in the center of the organs and energies it influences. Your sacral chakra is most often connected with sexual pleasure and fulfillment, but this is only the tip of the iceberg.

SACRAL CHAKRA ASSOCIATIONS

The sacral chakra is the root of your emotions. This is where your feelings develop, but also where they are used to fuel your creativity and your passion. The energy that flows through your sacral chakra adds spice and color to your life, enabling you to feel excited, joyful, and inspired.

When people associate the sacral chakra with passion, they commonly think of sexual passion, but that's only one aspect of it. Yes, your sacral chakra is all about pleasure, and your sexuality, sensuality, and even self-worth are all deeply affected by its influence, but it is also responsible for giving you a general passion for life. A lot of your identity and self-image is also rooted here—and why wouldn't they be? Your passions and emotions result in your individual expression that is unique to you.

Like all the chakras, your sacral chakra is also associated with some of the physical parts of your body, not just the emotional and spiritual side. Because of its position in your lower abdomen, it won't surprise you to hear that the sacral chakra has a strong influence on nearby organs, including your kidneys, bladder, and upper intestines. It also stimulates and regulates your sexual organs and bodily fluids—including your blood.

WHAT INFLUENCES THE SACRAL CHAKRA?

The sacral chakra's element is water—it does influence bodily fluids, after all—and this shows in the way it stimulates the flow of your emotions and creativity. When the chakra is balanced, you should find it easy to express your ideas and feelings, but if it isn't, you could find yourself with a case of writer's block or wildly fluctuating between different emotions. You can use this connection with water to help you balance your sacral chakra: try lying in a darkened room and listening to ocean or rain sounds or meditating next to a fountain, pond, or other water feature.

(Mercury)

The planet that casts its influence over the sacral chakra is Mercury. Mercury is a very cerebral planet with strong links to communication. It stimulates your ability to think through problems, make clear decisions, and assess all possible outcomes. Mercury also has strong influences on the arts and can increase your creativity.

(The Moon)

Another celestial body that you can tune into is the moon. The moon's orbit causes the ebb and flow of the oceans, moving large bodies of water with the force of its gravity. Because the sacral chakra is associated with water, and it is responsible for the well-being of the fluid within your own body, its connection with the moon is powerful. You can maximize the benefits of this connection by paying attention to the cycles of the moon and thinking about how the different phases mirror the flow of your own spiritual energy. Take extra moments of rest during new and full moons, and embrace the periods of change that are supported by the waning and waxing moons.

Your sacral chakra is also influenced by the Hindu goddess Parvati, also known as Uma. She is the goddess of love, devotion, and fertility, so it's no real surprise that she keeps watch over the chakra that rules your reproductive organs and your sexual desires. Parvati is usually depicted as kind, gentle, and maternal; exactly the kind of spirit you want as guardian of your emotions.

HOW TO KNOW IF YOUR SACRAL CHAKRA NEEDS HELP

Your sacral chakra is bright and inspiring, so when it is blocked or out of balance, you might feel like some of the light has left your life. This chakra is strongly influenced by the color orange—a color that is often associated with feelings of enthusiasm, optimism, and a desire to be creative. When your life energy cannot flow correctly through your sacral chakra, it can lead to emotional outbursts and general lethargy.

Other ways you can tell that your sacral chakra isn't working properly:

- You find it difficult to retain self-control in circumstances where you want something badly. This could result in strong cravings that you feel powerless to resist. It can start as something seemingly innocuous, such as eating and drinking too much, binge-watching tv, or finding it impossible to put down a video game, but it can also grow to include substance abuse or infidelity.

- Constant feelings of guilt and inadequacy that play havoc with your self-confidence. These can lead to self-punishing behavior, like refusing to acknowledge successes and denying yourself anything you enjoy. This often includes being frigid or reserved about your sexuality and not accepting that a healthy sex life is normal and fulfilling.

- The sacral chakra manages your emotions, and a blockage can mean that your emotions are no longer under control. Unexpected outbursts or quickly switching between emotions—being excited one minute and angry the next—usually indicates your life energy isn't nourishing this chakra.

- Remember, your sacral chakra influences your body parts too, and when it is blocked, this will manifest as physical symptoms. These include:
- Being prone to bladder infections, recurring cases of cystitis, and incontinence.
- Problems with infertility. These may be diagnosable issues like low sperm count and polycystic ovary syndrome, or they might just manifest as unspecified issues getting pregnant or taking longer than expected to conceive.
- Increased sensitivity to changing hormones during your menstrual cycle. Blocked sacral energy can mean that you experience strong PMS symptoms, such as cramps, nausea, night sweats, and emotional outbursts.
- Issues with your kidneys, including recurring kidney stones and infections. If your kidneys aren't working properly, it can affect how often you urinate, make you feel weak, and weaken your appetite.

USING HERBS TO UNBLOCK YOUR SACRAL CHAKRA

Eating orange foods is a really effective way of starting to recharge and unblock your sacral chakra in general. Sweet potatoes, pumpkins, mangos, oranges, and papayas are doubly effective because they are also juicy, meaning not only are you getting the benefits of orange food, but you're also connecting with the element of water.

Because a blocked sacral chakra can manifest in a number of different ways, you may want to choose the right herbs to help rather than looking for a generic solution. Some herbs have been proven to stimulate different areas of the body, but remember that spiritual herbalism acknowledges that not all plant spirits are compatible with all people. What works for one person may not help another, so make sure that you look for the right spiritual match as well as the herb that will help your symptoms. You might find that a certain herb seems to jump out at you: listen to what the plant spirits are trying to communicate because that herb might just be the one that supercharges your sacral chakra.

(Chaste tree berry)

HERBS FOR THE REPRODUCTIVE SYSTEM

If you need further proof of how valuable our relationship with plants is, then look no further than phytoestrogens. These are naturally occurring chemicals in a number of plants that mimic the animal hormone estrogen and can actually affect our bodies in the same way. If you have low estrogen levels, you might suffer from irregular or skipped periods, low sex drive, headaches, weight gain, and fatigue. Taking herbs that have a high concentration of phytoestrogens may counteract some of these problems because your body will react to them in the same way as it would to an increase in your natural estrogen levels (White, 2017). Recommended herbs include chaste tree berry, red clover, and cramp bark.

HERBS TO INCREASE YOUR LIBIDO

(*Maca Root*)

Adaptogenic plants and mushrooms work with your body to help fight against the negative effects of stress. These could be emotional or physical. Adaptogens work by restoring your body to its natural state, sort of like restoring your factory settings. Maca root is an incredible adaptogen. It grows in the Andes mountains and works as a natural aphrodisiac, as well as helping to keep your reproductive system in good working order. There have been small studies that show it actually increases sperm quality (Gonzales, 2012), as well as showing that maca root can help to combat a loss of libido post-menopause (Brooks et al., 2008).

HERBS TO CONNECT WITH YOUR SENSUAL SELF

Not all sexual dysfunctions are rooted in physical issues. Traumas that we suffer, whether physical or emotional, may result in us withdrawing from this aspect of ourselves. Stress, fatigue, and depression all lower your sex drive, and these, in turn, can lead to feelings of guilt and inadequacy as you wonder, what is wrong with me? Herbal aphrodisiacs can help to reconnect you with your sexual self by mini-

mizing some of these anxieties. For example, hawthorn heals a broken heart, while kava promotes openness and helps to quell inhibitions. Others, like maca root and damiana, work by stimulating your sexual organs, increasing blood flow, and regulating your sex hormones.

(Red Clover)

SACRAL CHAKRA HEALING WITH NATURE

Your sacral chakra is the root of your creativity, passion, and enjoyment of life, so it's one of the most important chakras to keep in balance. Because of its connection to water, it responds well to herbs taken as teas or tinctures. I've already mentioned a few herbs that can be used to target specific concerns, but the following herbs can be used more allopathically to target your sacral chakra itself. Some are available from the grocery store; others will be stocked by a good apothecary or herbalist. You might even want to try growing some yourself.

Damiana (Turnera Diffusa)

Damiana is a tall, flowering shrub native to Mexico but also found in Central America, the Caribbean, and the state of Texas. Its small, yellow flowers contrast with its dark green leaves, making it very distinctive. It flowers in the summer, and the flowers turn into fruit in the fall. Although the fruits are edible—in fact, they taste lovely and sweet and are often compared to figs—it is the leaves of the damiana plant that are harvested for medicinal use.

Because it grows in a warm climate, if you want to grow your own damiana plants, you will need to keep them in a heated and humid environment. Although the shrub can grow up to 6 ft tall, you don't need to wait that long and can start harvesting the leaves from your seedlings once they reach about 10 in tall.

The leaves and stalk were part of traditional religious ceremonies of the Guaycura people, who then traded their knowledge with the Mayans and Aztecs—they then started using damiana tonics as a general revitalizer and also as an aphrodisiac. The leaves are dried out and ground into a powder or milled, so they can be brewed into a tea. Drinking damiana tea is a popular way to absorb the benefits of this stimulating herb.

Several chemical compounds have been identified in and extracted from damiana, including a number of flavonoids like pinocembrin. The chemical that gives this herb its relaxing quality is apigenin—and it's this stress-relieving compound that can have an aphrodisiac effect.

Unsurprisingly, damiana is influenced by the planet Venus; ruler of joy, love, passion, and reproduction. This gives it an incredibly strong connection to your sacral chakra and your lust for life and love. Damiana is a dry, warming herb, so make sure you combine it with extra fluids or take it in its fluid form. You don't want to risk upsetting the fluid balance of your sacral chakra.

Damiana has several healing qualities that make it popular amongst herbalists. Damiana is a popular antidepressant and antianxiety medication due to its ability to help you relax. It has some mild psychotropic qualities that help people to get into a state of calm, forget what is making them stressed, and even shed some inhibitions. It is often used as an aphrodisiac for male sexual health for this very reason, as these effects can reduce problems associated with achieving and maintaining an erection. In women, it helps to relieve some of the negative symptoms of menopause.

Although it has many uses, damiana also has a number of possible side effects and contraindications that mean it isn't suitable for everybody. You should not take damiana if you are pregnant or breastfeeding; in fact, women should be careful taking it unless they know they have a hormonal imbalance because it increases testosterone. You should also avoid it if you have low blood sugar, as it could make you feel excessively tired.

Hibiscus (Hibiscus Sabdariffa)

(Hibiscus)

Hibiscus flowers are instantly recognizable by their large, red petals and long protruding stigma. It is native to Africa, originating in Angola and spreading north to other areas in Africa and Asia, including Egypt, Sudan, China, and Thailand. It's also farmed in areas of Central America and Mexico, and if you want to try growing it at home, you're going to need a similarly warm climate somewhere indoors. The flowers can be harvested over the winter, usually from October to March, and dried out to produce the ingredients for delicious hibiscus tea.

Although the whole flower is used when brewing hibiscus tea, the most beneficial part is actually the calyxes or sepals of the flower head—this is the part that protects the flower while it is still in its bud form. These calyxes are particularly rich in antioxidant compounds called polyphenols and anthocyanins. Anthocyanins are also a strong anti-inflammatory, making hibiscus doubly beneficial.

All over the world, people have known about its restorative qualities for thousands of years. Traditionally, hibiscus has been used as a tonic to help maintain normal levels of blood pressure, cholesterol, body temperature, body weight, and circulation. It has also been used externally as a topical ointment or cream. This is because hibiscus nourishes the skin and helps to clear your complexion. Hibiscus has also been used to nourish and restore health to your hair when used as a mask, revitalizing it and encouraging thicker, healthier hair to grow.

Because of its anti-inflammatory qualities, you won't be surprised to hear that hibiscus is considered a cooling herb. Drinking it as a warm tea can help to balance this effect if you already have a cool constitution. If you have a hot constitution, hibiscus is an excellent herb for drawing excess heat away from the body and might be beneficial as a daily tonic. Hibiscus is another herb working under the planetary correspondence of Venus, drawing healing energy for your kidneys and reproductive system and targeting the responsibilities of your sacral chakra.

Hibiscus is still used today as a general tonic, but scientists have also discovered that this herb boasts amazing anti-cancer properties. Not only can it slow down the growth of cancer cells, it actually stops some kinds of cancers from spreading at all.

Hibiscus is a powerful herb imbued with magical healing powers to counteract a number of conditions and imbalances all over the body. It is particularly effective at recharging the sacral chakra because of its strong alignment with the reproductive system, the kidneys, and the circulatory system. It's also an extremely safe herb with very few side effects. Anyone taking medication for diabetes or high blood pressure should consult with their doctor before taking hibiscus, but everyone else is able to enjoy its benefits freely.

CINNAMON (CINNAMOMUM ZEYLANCIUM)

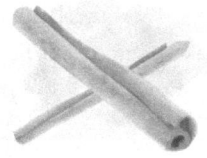

Most people might be familiar with cinnamon because

it's a common ingredient for baking everything from apple pie to spiced soup. You might even have some store-bought cinnamon sticks in the cupboard right now. The plant itself is native to Sri Lanka, a small island off the south coast of India, but it's also grown in the Caribbean, Brazil, India, and some of the South Pacific islands.

Cinnamon trees grow in sand and need a lot of rain and heat, making them very difficult to grow at home, but they are farmed and cultivated in large quantities by commercial growers. The trees have large, shiny, green leaves with small, white flowers sprinkled at the end of the branches. These eventually become bluish berries that taste similar to juniper berries. But the bit of the tree that is harvested as a spice and used for its medicinal qualities is the bark itself. Not the hard outer bark but younger inner layers from the smaller shoots.

Given where and how it grows, it's not surprising that cinnamon is ruled by the sun. Sun herbs play a strong role in maintaining your circulation and blood vessels, but they have emotional benefits, too: sun herbs help you find your rhythm and your natural flow and do a lot of work with your sense of self. Cinnamon is also a hot and dry herb, which is why it's often added to hot foods to add some spicy heat. When it heats the body, it helps to improve blood flow, warming and energizing your circulatory system.

Traditionally, cinnamon has been used as an oil in religious ceremonies. It's even mentioned in the Bible. Its warm, spicy smell is so distinctive that it was used by the Egyptians in their mummification rituals to preserve bodies and cover up their odor. Although cinnamon is easy to get hold of now, it used to be so valuable that very few people could afford it.

Cinnamon has some amazing anti-microbial properties that mean it's great at fighting off infections or any kind of bacterial or viral attack, like the common cold or a bout of winter flu. Adding cinnamon to tea, coffee, or hot chocolate will not only cheer up your taste buds but also give your immune system a boost when it's struggling.

Ever wondered why there are so many desserts and baked goods with cinnamon in them? This herb is great for your digestion because it calms down bloating and cramps, so it's the perfect way to end a meal. It even works for menstrual cramps—another good excuse to add it to your hot cocoa.

Cinnamon is safe to take in moderate to large doses, but it can cause some nasty side effects if you take too much. It's not recommended in medicinal doses if you are taking blood thinners, during pregnancy, or if you are prone to stomach ulcers.

Shatavari (Asparagus Racemosus)

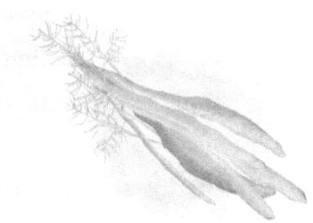

The name shatavari translates as 'having one hundred roots', and it's a great description of what goes on beneath the surface of this feathery plant. Although it looks a little like a wild carrot above the ground—long, thin, wispy leaves and little white flowers—under the ground, it produces a network of finger-like roots.

Shatavari grows in the wild in India and other parts of Asia with a tropical climate, but it's actually really hardy and will grow under a number of conditions. The better quality your soil is, the better root systems you will grow, so it's best to remove as many rocks and stones as possible before sowing. The plants grow slowly and are best harvested after at least 18 months. When you're ready to dig them up, take care not to pierce or damage the roots, as this is the best part of the herb. You can wash and peel the outer layer of the root, which will allow the inside to dry out quickly, so it can be ground for use.

Shatavari is an adaptogenic herb, meaning it is great for

helping your body recover from the effects of stress. Modern research has also proven that shatavari has anti-inflammatory and antioxidant qualities because it contains high quantities of racemofuran and saponins. This anti-inflammatory property means it is a cold herb, so if you have a cold constitution, you should take it in moderation.

Ayurvedic medicine has been using shatavari for thousands of years as a rejuvenating tonic for the female reproductive system. It was supposed to help protect against the effects of hormonal changes such as menopause. Practitioners would also prescribe shatavari as a tonic for the blood, hoping to combat different disorders and insufficiencies.

Nowadays, shatavari is used for a number of different purposes, not just to balance and restore your reproductive system. It also works as a general tonic, stimulating and supporting the digestive system, immune system, and raising your energy levels. Because shatavari is a cooling herb, it has a wonderfully gentle soothing effect on the body, which can be particularly useful in the event of an overstimulated sacral chakra.

Shatavari has been used for so long because it causes very few problems and side effects, making it a truly universal herb that can benefit everyone. Although ayurvedic practitioners maintain that it is safe to use while pregnant or breastfeeding, there hasn't been enough research into its use in these situations, so it might be best to avoid it. Because shatavari is a member of the asparagus family, anyone with an asparagus allergy should give it a wide berth. Do not take shatavari with other diuretic herbs or medication, as it can have a similar effect, and you don't want to end up accidentally doubling your dose.

RECIPES AND RELAXATION

Because your sacral chakra's element is water, these recipes use a lot of liquid. Your sacral chakra brings a lot of fluidity to your life, as well as inspiring your creative nature. These are both qualities that encourage you to play around and make changes that suit you, and that's exactly what I want to encourage you to do with these recipes. Swap out ingredients you don't fancy and replace them with other favorites; just remember to use herbs, fruits, and vegetables that are in tune with your sacral chakra.

HIBISCUS TEA

You can drink this gorgeous red tea hot or cold, sweetened or natural; it's really versatile, and there isn't one way that is the "right" way.

You will need:

- 1 cup of dried hibiscus flowers, or 4 cups of fresh flowers
- 2 liters of water

Simply pour the flowers into a large jug and add cold water. This will make a delicious cold brew that will need to steep overnight in your refrigerator. Once made, it will keep for up to five days, so you can take your time to enjoy it.

If you prefer your hibiscus tea hot, simply place 2 tsps of dried flowers in a cup and pour over freshly boiled water.

Hibiscus tea has a slightly tart or bitter flavor that some people like and others don't. You can add your choice of sweetener to balance out the taste.

Some great options are:

- honey
- mango juice
- maple syrup
- agave syrup
- strawberry juice
- pomegranate

For an extra boost to your sacral chakra, try adding a stick of cinnamon or a splash of fresh orange juice.

SACRAL BOOST SMOOTHIE

Juicy orange fruits with a high water content are exactly what your sacral chakra needs for a good tune-up, and this smoothie is full of them. Of course, you can mix and match with others, including passion-fruit, orange, grapefruit, and peaches.

You will need:

- a banana
- 1 cup of frozen mango
- 1 cup of fresh or frozen papaya
- ½ cup of frozen raspberries
- a pinch of cinnamon
- almond milk or a fruit yogurt

Blend all the solid ingredients together with the cinnamon. When everything is a smooth consistency, add the milk or yogurt to thin it out. If you fancy a tasty shake version of this smoothie, you could blend it with frozen yogurt instead.

Supercharge Your Sacral Soup

This filling soup is packed full of healing orange vegetables and warming spices that will help to open your sacral chakra and keep your life energy flowing freely. It's also super tasty. The recipe below makes four servings, so you can give your friends a boost too.

You will need:

- 1 tbsp of coconut oil
- 4 cloves of garlic, sliced
- 1 white onion, chopped
- 1 large sweet potato, peeled and chopped
- 4 carrots, peeled and chopped
- 800g of butternut squash, peeled and chopped
- 1.5 l of vegan chicken stock
- 1 tbsp of paprika
- 1 tbsp of cumin

Start by heating the coconut oil in a large saucepan or stock pot. Add the garlic and the onion and fry until soft. Add the carrots, sweet potato, and squash and stir together. Sprinkle over the spices and mix thoroughly. After a few minutes, you should pour in the stock and then bring everything to a boil. Turn down the heat and let it simmer for half an hour, then pour the contents into a blender and whizz until smooth. Serve immediately, garnished with a little thyme and a drizzle of olive oil.

SACRAL CHAKRA MEDITATION

Make sure you have a calm, quiet place where you can perform this meditation uninterrupted. Turn off your phone, draw the curtains, and dim the lights. Because the sacral chakra is attuned to the element of water, you could perform this meditation outside next to a pond or water feature for added spiritual energy. Another option is to have a soundtrack of ocean or rain sounds playing in the background. You can also burn some cinnamon incense sticks to utilize your sense of smell in the healing process. Alternatively, mix a potpourri bowl of dried hibiscus, orange rose petals, and cinnamon chips.

It's important to focus your energy on your sacral chakra, so find a position to sit in where your hips are slightly above your knees. A good way to do this is by sitting on the floor with your legs crossed and placing a couple of pillows or rolled-up towels under your buttocks. Rock your pelvis forward and backward to loosen everything up before settling into your neutral position.

Close your eyes and imagine a beautiful ocean sunset. The glowing orange sun is just beginning to dip below the horizon as the waves gently lap against the shore. Focus on the waves and try to align your breathing with their movement: breathe in as the waves climb the sand and breathe out as they return to the ocean. You could use the yogic technique of ujjayi breathing (nasal breathing in and out with shut lips, mimicking ocean wave sounds with your constricted throat) here to mimic the sounds of the waves. This is a great way to release stress and tension from your body. Imagine any stiffness or stress being swept out to sea and carried far away.

On your final five exhalations, chant the syllable *vam*. Slowly open your eyes and stretch your legs out in front of you. Give the blood flow a chance to stabilize before getting up, or you might feel a little light-headed.

3

THE SOLAR PLEXUS CHAKRA

Your third chakra, the Solar Plexus chakra or Manipura, can be found close to the literal center of your body. Above your navel and below your breastbone, it inhabits the space around your stomach and liver - two organs over which it has a strong influence.

As your chakras move up your body, they start to become less concerned with the purely physical elements of your being and instead have more influence over not only your own spiritual energy but also how you connect with the energy around you.

SOLAR PLEXUS CHAKRA ASSOCIATIONS

Your Solar Plexus chakra contains the very essence of your being. The energy that passes through it powers your sense of self and dictates how you see yourself fitting in with the world. If this chakra is working correctly, you will feel confident and motivated. You will be aware of your purpose in life and know how you can strive towards it. You will also be aware of how you can grow, both emotionally and spiritually, and be able to set yourself clear goals and boundaries to make sure you can attain this high awareness.

Another important quality associated with your solar plexus chakra is that it is the center of your intuition—literally, your gut feelings. When you have a hunch about something or feel an inexplicable desire to refuse an offer, you are listening to the wisdom of this chakra. Being the seat for your true self and your true desires also means the solar plexus chakra is the seat of individualized wisdom; the decisions that are best for you. If you are attuned to this chakra, you can't go wrong in life.

The idea of transformation corresponds strongly with the actions of this chakra, both physically and spiritually. On the one hand, your solar plexus chakra encourages you to grow into your best self, to transform from matter and energy into a fully realized being. On the other hand, it is responsible for some of the major bodily organs that transform food into energy: your stomach, kidneys, and liver.

Your solar plexus chakra is the final chakra to correspond with the waxing moon—yet another example of this chakra's link with transformation. The waxing moon is highly energized, symbolizing new growth and the emergence of light from darkness. It encourages you to shed your fears and grow into your potential, realizing your full self and all you are capable of.

WHAT INFLUENCES THE SOLAR PLEXUS CHAKRA?

The color associated with this chakra is yellow, which symbolizes joy, courage, and the energy of youth. This bright color is filled with positive energy and has a stimulating, energizing effect on your energy body. Your solar plexus chakra is also associated with the element of fire, another important form of energy. This fire energy lights up your digestive system, although too much of it can have an adverse effect, causing inflammation and indigestion. Fire can be a difficult element to control, which is why there are so many herbalist tonics and tinctures designed to regulate your digestive system. I've included a few at the end of this chapter that can help to keep your solar plexus chakra's element in balance.

(*The Sun*)

Your solar plexus chakra is ruled by the sun, another great source of fiery energy. The sun is the center of our solar system, and your solar plexus chakra echoes this by not only being the center of your body but by influencing the core of your being: your identity or your ego. Another guardian of your solar plexus chakra is the Hindu goddess Lakshmi. She is the goddess of wealth and fortune, and when combined with your solar plexus chakra, this is interpreted as spiritual and emotional wealth rather than physical.

The sense associated with the solar plexus chakra is sight, so it draws healing energy from color therapy as well as the herbs you take. For this reason, when you want to work on unblocking or strengthening this chakra, it's always a good idea to have yellow plants to hand. Daffodils and yellow tulips work wonders because they are both symbolic of the transition between winter and springtime, and they spiritually embody pure transformational energy. Having these plants in your home is also uplifting and cheering, as their bright colors are capable of bringing a smile to your face any time of day.

HOW TO KNOW IF YOUR SOLAR PLEXUS CHAKRA NEEDS HELP

Your solar plexus chakra holds the key to your personality and identity; if something is wrong, it will manifest in negative behaviors and a lack of confidence. An imbalance here will allow fear to seep into your spiritual core, and that can lead to self-doubt and blocked communication between your brain and your gut. Those gut feelings we talked about earlier? They are a crucial part of your spiritual awareness, and they allow you to experience the world on a different level from your conscious thoughts. When you stop listening to them or stop trusting them, it damages your connection with the universe.

Other signs of an unbalanced chakra include:

- Becoming aggressive and controlling. People with an overactive solar plexus chakra have too much fire energy feeding their ego, and they may become demanding and might try to force their will onto the universe and others.

- Not thinking of others, blaming others when things go wrong, and refusing to accept accountability. This chakra helps you understand your place in the world, and when it isn't working properly, you may lose sight of that. Someone who is spiritually disconnected is only capable of seeing themselves, and this is reflected by their selfish and self-centered behavior.

- Approval-seeking behavior and a lack of willpower. If your chakra is blocked and you're unable to connect to the universe's energy flow, you can end up feeling isolated and alone. This leaves you over-reliant on the opinions of others to find your place, and you can be easily led by their desires rather than your own.

- If the energy flow through your solar plexus chakra is blocked or disturbed, it can also cause physical problems with the organs and systems that are aligned with this chakra.

- Digestive upsets are common with a blocked chakra. The energy flowing through your stomach, liver, and kidneys works to clean away emotional impurities, and if these build up, they can cause irritation and inflammation, often leading to indigestion, stomach ulcers, and trapped gas.

- Your liver holds on to a lot of repressed anger and bitterness. Without the cleansing energy of a well-balanced chakra, these emotions can build up and manifest as liver disease.

TUNING YOUR DIGESTIVE SYSTEM

When most people think of the digestive system, they picture the stomach and intestines, but it is actually a lot more than that. It is one long tube from your mouth, down your throat, through your stomach and intestines, and ending at your anus. It also involves separate organs like your liver, gallbladder, and pancreas.

Everything you eat or drink, as well as a whole lot of stuff that gets in by accident, has to go through your digestive system. Along the way, your body extracts all the nutrients and goodness, filters out the toxins, and then removes the waste products. This does mean that your digestive tract is more easily affected by issues, especially if you eat too much processed food, uncooked food with bacteria, or drink excessive amounts of alcohol: These all put extra strain on your digestion to remove the unwanted elements, leaving your stomach, liver, and intestines vulnerable and overworked.

Making sure you eat a diet rich in fiber will help to stop physical blockages, but you also need to think about emotional and spiritual blockages. Your gut is strongly tied to intuition, and gut feelings come from a place of openness and spiritual awareness in your solar plexus chakra. If this chakra is sluggish and blocked, you will be less open to the messages of the universe, and your gut feelings will be off.

YOUR LIVER AND ANGER

Different emotions are seated in different parts of your body, but this is probably something you already unconsciously knew. Think about different feelings and where they are felt: anxiety and worry tend to churn your stomach, whereas fear causes a tightening in your chest. Joy and happiness are tied to your solar plexus chakra, filling your abdomen with warmth, and anger is connected with your liver, meaning it can cause some disruption to your digestion if it isn't expressed effectively.

Anger is one of the most misunderstood emotions. Today's society tells us that expressing anger is wrong, so we tend to bottle it up and repress our angry feelings. But anger is a useful, primal emotion, and it protects us from spiritual and emotional harm. When something makes us feel angry, it can give us the energy to fight back and stand up for what we believe is right. This is one way we can express our anger in a productive and healthy manner. But too much-suppressed anger can be poisonous: it will attack the liver, causing damage and disease, or it can explode in an uncontrolled outburst, leaving us to pick up the pieces afterward.

Your liver is in correspondence with Jupiter, the planet of wisdom and generosity. Like Jupiter, the liver gives more to the body than it takes, working tirelessly to remove physical and emotional toxins to keep your digestive system—and your whole body—clean and purified. It is also an energizing organ, and if it's damaged or stagnating, you will find yourself feeling lethargic and fatigued.

An imbalance in your liver, or a blockage preventing its energy from flowing freely, won't always be felt in your abdomen. There is an energy link between this area and your brain called the gut-brain axis, and often symptoms in one will relate to an issue in the other. If your brain is worrying about something, you feel it manifest as butterflies in your stomach, and a surge of anger from your liver can cause a headache.

Some other signs that your liver is out of balance include:

- Grinding your teeth or clenching your jaw. This often has the secondary effect of causing a headache due to overworked muscles.

- Tightness in the muscles around your neck and shoulders. These areas can hold a lot of stress, especially when it's caused by repressed emotions.
- Feeling irritable and quick to anger. You might feel like you're constantly at the end of your tether, and even the littlest things can cause an unwarranted outburst.

You can help to stimulate your liver by adding plenty of fresh fruit and vegetables to your diet, especially leafy greens like cabbage, broccoli, and kohlrabi. The liver also responds well to herbs like rosemary, basil, and watercress. Beware of eating too many spicy foods and herbs, as these can irritate rather than stimulate.

DIGESTIVE AND SOLAR PLEXUS CHAKRA HEALING WITH NATURE

When your solar plexus chakra is out of balance, you often suffer from an excess of fire energy. This means you'll need gentle, calming, and cooling herbs in order to restore balance and restore the natural flow of your life force through your energy body. The core belief of spiritual herbalism is that herbs work best for us if we have a spiritual connection with them, so you should take your time experimenting with different herbs until you find one that speaks to you. Listen to the universe and ask for guidance because you might find yourself directed to a specific plant if you pay attention.

The solar plexus chakra is linked to the element of fire, and you'll find that the following herbs mainly act in a cooling way to restore balance when your chakra is overactive. Excess fire energy leads to uncomfortable digestive issues like cramps, indigestion, bloating, and gas, but a quick sip of some herbal teas and tonics is often all you need to feel yourself again. These herbs can be grown or wildcrafted in most countries, or you should be able to find them in a good health store.

FENNEL (FOENICULUM VULGARE)

This tall shrub can be found growing wild in most of Europe, especially in coastal regions, and also along the coasts of California, where it is thought of as a troublesome weed. Fennel grows quickly and is extremely hardy, making it difficult to get rid of once it sets up at home. You can recognize it by its tall green stalks and blooms of tiny yellow flowers that spread like the head of a makeup brush.

You can grow fennel easily at home, and the best time to sew it is in the spring. Plant it somewhere it can enjoy the sunlight and keep it in moist but well-drained soil. Your plants should flower in July and August. Fennel is an amazing herb because the whole plant can be used. The bulb and leaves are used in cooking, and the seeds have medicinal uses. Try adding fennel leaves to a salad or using the stalks to bulk up soups and stews. The bulbs are delicious when roasted.

Fennel is a very mild herb and can be used by children as well as adults. In fact, it has been used for many years as a cure for colic and trapped gas in babies and toddlers. It was also traditionally used by breastfeeding mothers to help increase their milk supply.

Nowadays, fennel is used in a number of different ways to treat digestive and intestinal issues. It has antispasmodic properties, so it is wonderful for relieving cramps. Because it has such a gentle formula, it is safe for long-term use, making it hugely beneficial to those suffering from chronic conditions like IBS and Crohn's Disease.

Mercury casts its astral influence over Fennel and imbues this herb with its calming qualities. Fennel is also a cooling herb, as demonstrated by its ability to quell the fires of indigestion caused by an overactive solar plexus chakra. Its distinctive and pleasant aniseed flavor makes it an ideal herb to use in combination with other, less palatable options. The seeds also make an excellent tea that can be drunk hot or enjoyed cold.

Fennel should not be taken in medicinal doses if you are pregnant or suffer from estrogen-sensitive conditions. In its essential oil form, fennel can stimulate the nervous system, so if you already have a condition of the nervous system, it is best avoided. Otherwise, fennel is a very gentle, soothing, and calming herb that can be used to medicate both adults and children.

Peppermint (Mentha Piperita)

This is one of the herbs that people are most familiar with, as it is the basis for the refreshing minty flavor in a lot of toothpaste and dental products, as well as peppermint candies. The peppermint plant can be found growing wild all over Europe and North America, where it has made itself very much at home. Its unique scent makes it easy to identify, along with its jagged green leaves and tiny red flowers.

Peppermint is easily scavenged but not so easily grown at home. It rarely produces fertile seeds, so seedlings are cultivated by taking cuttings from mature plants. However, if you purchase established shrubs, this herb will happily make itself at home in any temperate garden. Peppermint also grows well inside as a windowsill herb, which means you can benefit from the lovely aroma given off by its leaves. Harvest the leaves in summer and fall, and then cut back the plant over the winter to ensure it will grow again next year.

The distinctive peppermint smell is made by the oil that can be distilled from the plant's leaves. This oil is mostly made of menthol, which is what gives peppermint its cooling properties. Once extracted, this oil is used to flavor or dilute into a tincture of its own. Historically, peppermint has been used in cooking and medicine for thousands of years. It has been known as a remedy for stomach ailments because it reduces cramps and eases indigestion. It also helps when you're feeling sick and was a popular remedy for travel sickness. Its cooling nature also made it an obvious choice for dealing with fever and helping to soothe and calm anyone who was suffering from sweating and overheating.

Peppermint is associated with the element of air and the planet Venus. Both promote the idea of restoration and rejuvenation, with air blowing away blockages and breathing new life into your spiritual energy. Anyone who has ever enjoyed a double-strength mint will know that menthol is absolutely capable of blowing out the cobwebs and giving you a burst of clarity.

Nowadays, peppermint is still used to calm an upset stomach, relieve bloating, and help to combat feelings of nausea. It's also used as a decongestant for people suffering from colds and flu and to remedy the high temperatures brought on by a fever. It is also used as a cream to soothe inflamed skin. Peppermint is generally well-tolerated by everyone, but it shouldn't be taken in large doses when breastfeeding as it can affect one's milk supply.

CHAMOMILE (MATRICARIA CHAMOMILLA)

There are several different types of chamomile plants, and the variant most often used in modern herbalism is called German Chamomile. You will find these plants all over; they are native to Europe, Africa, and Asia and now grow in North America as well after being imported by early settlers. Chamomile makes a lovely garden plant, sprouting carpets of cheerful white daisy flowers every summer. The plants will grow in well-drained soil and prefer a sunny position. Sow seeds in May to harvest flowers in August.

German chamomile isn't actually a true chamomile plant, although it actually produces the same chemicals and oils as common chamomile but in larger quantities. This is why it is used by herbalists. It looks and smells the same as all the other chamomile plants and works just as well in all recipes. The white flowers are where it holds its power. Once harvested, these are dried and used for chamomile tea, or you can eat them fresh in a salad.

You can find chamomile growing wild, but because there are so many different variants and they all look almost identical, it can be difficult for even experienced herbalists to know which is which by sight alone. One good way is to smell the flowers; German chamomile and common chamomile both smell faintly of apples. If you spot this smell, you know you've found yourself a good herb bush. Remember not to damage any plants you are harvesting from; only take a small amount of the flowers, and give your thanks to the plant spirits for their gift.

Chamomile is a cooling herb that grows under the influence of the moon. The moon is all about regulating and nourishing, and it is particularly attuned to our digestive systems. This lunar energy infuses chamomile with wonderful benefits for your solar plexus chakra while its cooling nature acts to reduce inflammation and soothe disturbances. Chamomile has been used for thousands of years as a digestive tonic and is one of the few herbs gentle enough to be used by children.

Externally, chamomile lotions and balms make excellent salves for scrapes and rashes. You'll often find chamomile oil listed as an ingredient in modern lip balms and sugar scrubs because it is so soothing and restorative. Chamomile can be drunk as a tea or a tincture to help settle digestive issues, whether they are caused by something you ate or something you are worried about. In fact, chamomile is a wonderful way to calm nerves and anxieties, especially when your self-worth is thrown off by a blocked solar plexus chakra.

Because chamomile is a calming herb, it can be used to relax before bed and encourage a healthy night's sleep. This is especially useful for babies and infants, and a chamomile bath can help them drift off to a restful slumber. Bad reactions to chamomile are rare, but if you have an allergy to ragweed, it should be avoided.

LIVER HEALING WITH NATURE

It's so easy for your liver to become blocked, so I have included here some herbs that are specifically associated with this important organ. These can be used in addition to the general herbs listed above. It's always good to rotate the herbs you take as your body will become accustomed to them, and this weakens their effect, so the more herbs you have to choose from, the better.

Milk Thistle (Silybum Marianum)

Milk thistle is known as a hepatic herb, meaning it specifically targets its support towards the liver. It helps to protect liver function as well as prevent damage caused by free radical cells. You can use it to support the liver healing from any existing problems or as a general preventative.

Like all thistles, this herb is spiky in appearance, with an eye-catching purple flower. It's a perfect herb for wild-crafting because it is technically classed as a weed and can be found growing wild in rocky scrubland. Commercial milk thistle is cultivated on large plantations that can cope with its rapid spread; if you want to grow it in your garden, you must be careful to contain it because your neighbors won't thank you if it gets out. This means harvesting all the heads before the seeds drop, which will usually be in late May.

This is another herb where all parts of the plant have their uses. The roots and leaves can be cooked and eaten, and the flowers and stems are often brewed into teas. But the most beneficial parts are the seeds. These contain the chemical silymarin, which is what directly benefits your liver.

Milk thistle has been used as a liver remedy for hundreds of years, not only as a general tonic but also in the treatment of diseases like jaundice. It is influenced by the planet Jupiter, which also has an alignment with the liver; with so much planetary and spiritual energy focused toward one organ, it's no wonder that Milk Thistle is one of the most effective hepatic herbs you can choose. It is also known for its cooling nature, which means it is full of anti-inflammatory properties.

Tonics containing milk thistle are often recommended by herbalists to support a liver that has a serious existing condition, e.g., hepatitis, cirrhosis, enlargement of the liver, or issues due to excessive alcohol consumption. It works to protect the liver from further damage, as well as help repair and rebuild the liver cells themselves. Milk thistle is a great herb to use in the spring because of its rejuvenating qualities. It connects well with the season of renewal and is extra effective at this time.

Milk thistle has been known to interact with several prescription drugs, so you should never take it alongside long-term medication without checking with your doctor first. It is such a strong herb that it even flushes out the chemicals that you want in your body! It should also be avoided during pregnancy.

Astragalus Root (Astragalus Membranaceus)

This herb is native to China and Mongolia and has been used in traditional Chinese medicine for thousands of years. It has a reputation as a helper for your immune system, but it also works to repair and restore the liver. Astragalus root has antifibrotic properties that can prevent liver scarring, thereby acting as a shield against the damaging effects of liver disease. It is an adaptogen, meaning it adapts to help the body in different ways.

The astragalus plant will grow comfortably in a temperate climate and makes a beautiful addition to any garden. It can grow up to 4 ft tall and break out in small, yellow flowers that hang delicately from its long, green stalks. Astragalus grows best in well-drained, slightly sandy soil and prefers to be kept in partial shade. The root is the part of the herb that you want to use, and it can take two years for each plant to grow enough to be worth harvesting.

Astragalus is another herb that corresponds to Jupiter, underlining its influence over the liver. It is also associated with the element of air, which is why it is so stimulating for your sacral chakra. Air is necessary for fire to thrive, so by taking air herbs, you are feeding the fire element of your sacral chakra. Astragalus is a warming herb used to revive your energy levels and stimulate your body to repair itself. People with a hot constitution should avoid taking excessive amounts or might want to combine it with something cooling like chamomile.

The pharmacological constituents of astragalus that make it effective for treating so many different conditions are flavonoids and polysaccharides. Flavonoids search out and remove free radicals, which can prevent the development of heart disease, liver disease, and cancer. Polysaccharides are anti-inflammatory and antiviral, meaning they're great at clearing out infections and calming down irritations across the body. Because astragalus is an adaptogen, these qualities don't just target one organ but can have the same effect over many. It's a very handy herb to have in your collection, and you can benefit from taking it regularly as a preventative and general tonic.

Because astragalus root affects the immune system, people with autoimmune conditions shouldn't take it without first seeking medical advice. It is also not suitable for anyone who is pregnant or breastfeeding, as it might pass to the child in toxic amounts.

Barberry Root (Berberis Vulgaris)

The barberry herb has been used for medicinal purposes for over 2,500 years, treating everything from conjunctivitis to jaundice. It is native to Central Asia, North Africa, the Middle East, and parts of Europe, but some varieties also grow wild in the US. This plant is unusual in that the best time to sow seeds is over the winter months, and if you plan on growing them indoors, you'll need to start them in your refrigerator. Outdoor plants need to be protected from direct sunlight in warmer areas because it can scorch the leaves, so it's a good idea to keep the plants somewhere where they have a mixture of sun and shade.

Barberry bushes are extremely hardy and make colorful hedgerows, so people love to plant them along their property lines. The leaves change color with the seasons and look spectacular in their fall shades, which complement their stall cherry-red berries. You can eat the berries–they are juicy and tart-like cranberries—but the best part of this herb is the root.

The root contains an alkaloid chemical called berberine, which has many wonderful healing qualities. It is anti-inflammatory and antimicrobial and acts as a sedative to calm down heightened emotions, like the anger that can stem from a stagnant liver. Barberry root also specifically targets its healing towards the liver by stimulating it to produce more bile. This bile is really important for removing cholesterol and other contaminants from your system; without the bile to remove them, they will stay and block the liver, contaminating its energy.

Unlike other herbs that target the liver, barberry is not ruled by Jupiter but by Mars. This planet is strongly linked with the emotion of anger, and its placement in your chart can help you learn how to better redirect your anger towards beneficial pursuits. Barberry does the same thing with your liver, targeting the energy blockages that can cause anger to build up and restoring balance. It is also a drying and heating herb that works in partnership with the fire element of the solar plexus chakra.

Some variants of barberry are poisonous, so you might want to only get your barberry from specialist herbalist stores. You may want to refrain from wildcrafting barberry, as it's difficult to be 100% that the variety you picked isn't toxic. Even safe barberry plants can be toxic in large doses, so you should consult with a qualified herbalist before attempting home remedies. Barberry should never be taken during pregnancy or by infants. It also reacts badly with some long-term medications, so if you currently take any other medication, you must consult with your doctor before taking barberry supplements.

RECIPES TO REVIVE YOUR SOLAR PLEXUS CHAKRA

Calming Chamomile Oat Bath

There's no better way to relax at the end of the day than with a herbal bath. This one is safe for all members of the family and will help to soothe sores, chicken pox, rashes, and any other problems that are keeping little ones awake. Inhaling the warm scent of the chamomile will help your whole body to relax, and you'll soon feel your troubles melting away. This is a great way to soothe away your troubles and help you find your spiritual center.

You will need:

- an old sock
- 1 cup of oats
- ½ cup of dried chamomile flowers or 1 cup of fresh flowers
- ½ cup of dried lavender

Fill the sock with the oats, chamomile, and lavender.

Run your bath hotter than normal and add the sock—like a tea bag, it will infuse the bath water with the goodness of the herbs within! Swirl the water periodically as you wait for it to cool. Once the water has reached an acceptable temperature, climb in, lean back, and enjoy this relaxing herbal bath. You can even use the sock as a herbal scrub to exfoliate your skin or to target problem areas.

GAS-BE-GONE DIGESTIVE TONIC

This wonderful tonic is really easy and simple to make and uses three different herbs that are tuned into your solar plexus chakra. Take it before meals to help prevent bloating and gas build-up if you know you have a sensitive stomach. Alternatively, you can take it between meals if you start to feel bloated. You'll need to plan ahead, though, because this magic cure takes two weeks to mature.

You will need:

- 1 large tbsp of peppermint leaves (dried)
- 1 large tbsp of fennel seeds
- 1 in. piece of ginger root (chopped)
- 1 cup of apple cider vinegar

Blend all the ingredients until the liquid is as smooth as

you can get it. Pour it into a sterilized glass jar and seal it, then wrap the jar in a dark towel and store it in the back of a kitchen cabinet or pantry for two weeks.

Once your mixture has finished maturing, you'll need to strain out the solid particles. Use a fine mesh or a piece of cheesecloth and press the mixture through—don't forget to catch your liquid in another container. You will want to store this tincture in dark brown bottles and keep it away from the light. Mix 1 tsp with a ¼ cup of water and take this tonic before or after meals.

ENERGY BOOSTING *Solar Plexus Smoothie*

 Fruits are great for boosting your digestive system because they are full of fiber, and we all know that fiber is good for gut health. This simple smoothie works well as a quick breakfast to give you some slow-release energy and an essential burst of fiber, getting your day off to a great start.

You will need:

- 1 ripe banana
- 1 cup of fresh or frozen pineapple chunks
- ½ cup of vanilla yogurt
- 1 cup of almond or cashew nut milk
- ½ cup of ice chips

Blend everything for 40-60 seconds or until you get a smooth consistency. Pour into a tall glass and enjoy immediately. This is also a great post-workout tonic, as bananas are full of electrolytes and can replace those lost through sweating.

RECIPES TO AID THE LIVER

Liver Detoxing Tincture

Your liver does a fabulous job of removing toxins from your body, and this simple tincture can help to make sure that it never feels overburdened. If your liver is feeling overworked, you can pep it up again by taking a few drops before each meal.

You will need:

- 1 oz milk thistle seeds, ground
- ½ oz dandelion root, dried
- ½ oz burdock root, dried
- ½ oz turmeric root, dried
- 12 oz 100-proof alcohol

Place the herbs into a jar and pour the alcohol over the top. Screw the lid on tight and give it a good shake. Store it in a dark place, like the back of your kitchen cabinet or pantry. You'll need to leave it to steep for four weeks, but keep shaking it every three or four days to keep mixing up the contents.

When the tincture is ready, strain it through a fine mesh or a piece of cheesecloth so you are left with just the liquid. You can then store this in a clean jar somewhere away from direct sunlight.

ANTIOXIDANT TEA

The herbs in this recipe are full of antioxidants that will help combat free radicals, which can lead to liver disease. It's not only a great tonic for your liver, but it's also super tasty. This recipe makes two cups, so you can share the health benefits with a friend.

You will need:

- 2 tbsp of milk thistle seeds
- 1 tbsp of fresh ginger, sliced
- 3 cups of water

Set the water on the stove and let it boil. Add the ginger and simmer the mixture for ten minutes. The water should go pale yellow as the ginger cooks. While you wait, you'll need to crush the milk thistle seeds with a pestle and mortar. If you haven't got one, you could use the back of a metal spoon or the end of a rolling pin. Pour the water, ginger, and seeds into your teapot and leave to brew for five minutes. Strain the tea into a pair of mugs and enjoy.

Immune Boosting Astragalus Tea

This dual-function fruity tea will not only work to protect your liver—thanks to the astragalus root and red raspberry leaf —it is also brimming with important vitamins and minerals that will supercharge your immune system and keep you healthy. Some of the herbs are a little harder to find than others, but this tea works well no matter what combination of ingredients you manage to get together.

You will need:

- 2 parts elderberries, dried
- 1 part nettle, dried
- 1 part red raspberry leaf, dried
- 1 part oatstraw, dried
- 2 astragalus root strips
- 1 cinnamon stick

Put all the dried herbs together in a bowl and mix them really well. You can make as much of this tea blend as you like and store it for later: just make sure you have an airtight container to keep it in. Add the astragalus root strips and the cinnamon stick to a pot and add 4 tbsps of your herb mixture. Pour over enough boiling water for four cups, cover the pot, and let the tea steep.

To get the full benefits from your blend, leave it for four hours, but if you want it quickly, you can drink it after half an hour. Strain the tea when you're ready and reheat, or add ice for a refreshing summer blend. If you want to sweeten the tea, you can add some honey or stevia.

SOLAR PLEXUS CHAKRA MEDITATION

Perform this meditation at a time when you are feeling calm and relaxed—perhaps after a calming chamomile oat bath. For extra spiritual energy, perform this meditation by candlelight. Sit in a high-backed chair where your spine can lengthen, and your solar plexus chakra is held in the middle distance between your head and your feet. You might find it relaxing to burn some essential oils or place them in a nearby diffuser. Oils that are beneficial for the solar plexus chakra include those made from the herbs lavender, myrrh, cedarwood, and clary sage.

- Once you're sitting comfortably, close your eyes and visualize a warming fire igniting around your naval. Imagine it heating your stomach, liver, and kidneys, softening them, and melting away stiffness or impurities. Use ujjayi breath (as briefly described in the sacral chakra meditation) to exhale these impurities while warming and energizing your body.

- Place your right hand over your abdomen and gently massage in large, clockwise circles. This will start to loosen your stomach muscles and promote relaxation. You might enjoy rubbing a chamomile or mint lotion into your skin while you do this, adding cooling herbs to balance warmth from within.

- When you're ready to finish, chant the syllable *ram* on your final five exhalations. Open your eyes and try to retain the feeling of warmth in your abdomen. You should feel relaxed and free from stress and anger, and your digestive system will feel warm and energized.

This meditation can be particularly effective after you've eaten a rich evening meal to prevent indigestion from interfering with your sleep.

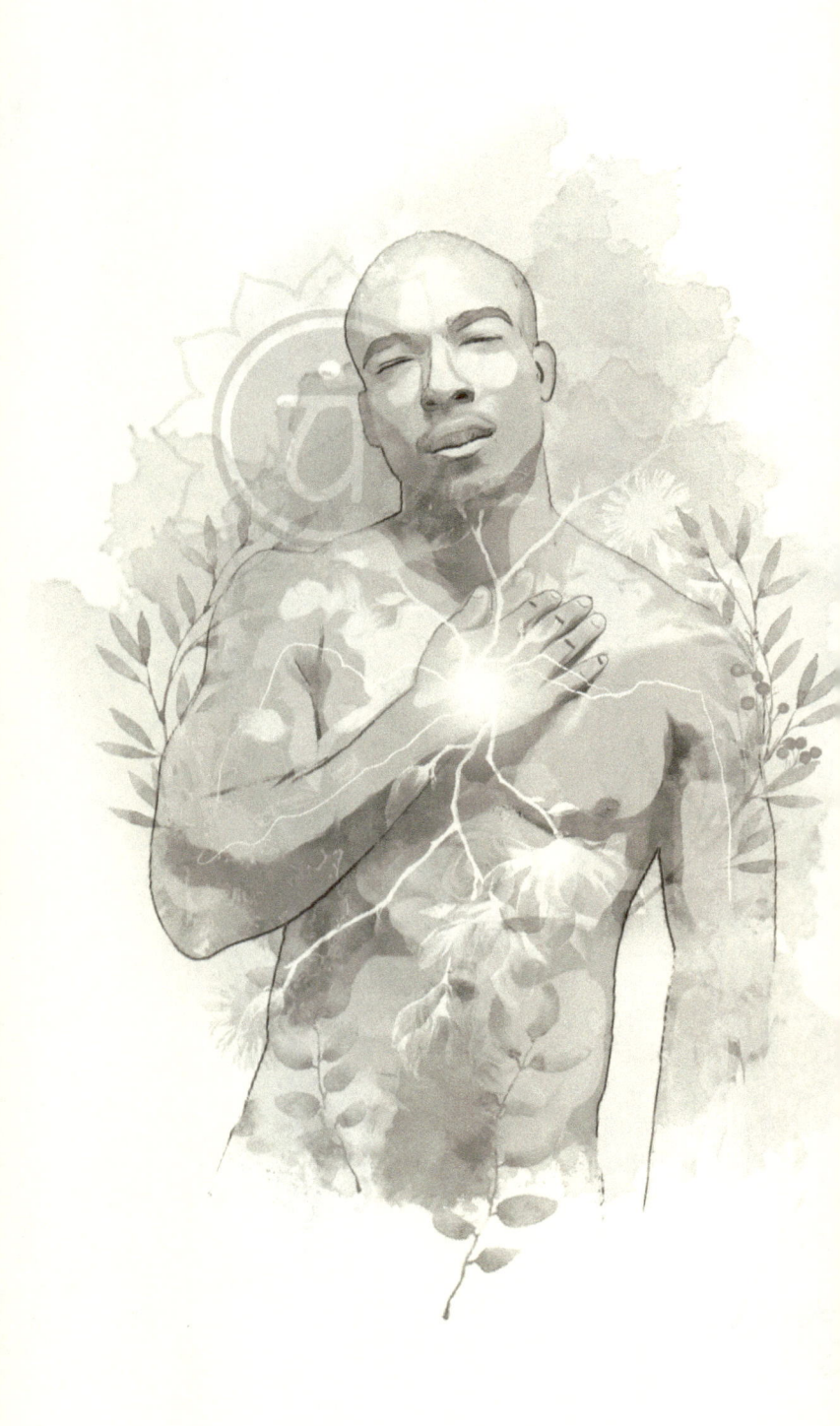

❦ 4 ❦
THE HEART CHAKRA

Your fourth chakra is located in the center of your chest, between your breastbone and your shoulder blades. The heart chakra, also known as Anahata, not only watches over your physical heart and its circulatory system, but it also houses your emotional heart.

Sitting directly above the solar plexus chakra, the overwhelmingly positive emotions of the heart chakra balance out the solar plexus chakra's potentially negative emotions. Your chakras do not function in isolation; rather, they are part of a constant ebb and flow of energy between the different wheels. Imagine a river flowing between different pools: it's impossible that some elements from one pool won't be transferred into the next. Any problems with lower chakras will also unbalance those above them, so before any healing of the heart chakra can occur, you must take the time to center and balance the three chakras below it.

Once you have started to address imbalances in the

three lower chakras, you can start to work on unblocking your heart chakra. The higher up the chakras you go, the more they are influenced by the spiritual nature of the herbs, as well as by their chemicals and properties. Now more than ever, it's important to try and source whole-spectrum herbal supplements and dried herbs, as these contain more of the original plant than just the active constituent. Using whole plants guarantees you a deeper connection to the plant spirits that will restore your energy to its rightful equilibrium.

HEART CHAKRA ASSOCIATIONS

Your heart chakra isn't just associated with your circulatory system; it also corresponds to your upper spine, shoulders, arms, hands, and respiratory system—your lungs, diaphragm, and blood (because it carries oxygen around the body). These organs are some of the most vital for life, so your heart chakra bears the weight of responsibility for your life itself. On the spiritual side, your heart chakra also guards the spark of your life energy housed within your spiritual heart. Without this, you would lose your lust for life and fade away.

The love you feel for yourself and others has its roots in your heart chakra. If it is nourished and open, you will be overwhelmed by kindness and compassion, but when it is blocked, you might find yourself feeling bitter, jealous, and possessive. All types of love reside in your heart chakra, along with other feelings that are linked to them. This includes your ability to trust others, your capacity for forgiveness, and your optimism and hope.

The heart chakra is one of the easiest chakras to nourish spiritually. The world, Mother Nature, and other people are filled with love, and this chakra is primed to receive that. When practicing spiritual herbalism, regardless of what herbs you take and where they are supposed to target, by opening yourself to Mother Nature and accepting her gifts, you are opening yourself to receiving her love. Thus, your heart chakra receives the benefits every time you thank the plant spirits and show your respect for Mother Nature and her gifts.

WHAT INFLUENCES THE HEART CHAKRA?

The heart chakra is heavily influenced by the element of air. It flows through your lungs, bringing with it renewed life and taking away toxins. Air is energizing and invigorating, and it symbolizes infinite possibilities. Once something is carried by the wind, there is no limit to how far it can go, and the same is true of love and compassion. True love gifted will be paid forward, and a small kindness today can create ripples that reach further than you ever imagined.

(*Venus*)

With so much centered around the heart and love, it's unsurprising that the heart chakra corresponds to the planet Venus. Venus rules over love and compassion with a gentle spirit, and the planetary energy we reap is all about joy and harmony. Of course, romantic love is nurtured here, but that is just one element. Love for your family and friends, respect for others, and compassion for strangers all draw their strength from Venus and your heart chakra. Most importantly of all, this chakra powers the love you have for yourself.

The Hindu deity associated with the heart chakra is Hanuman, a figure known for his devotion and commitment. The love he feels for Rāma and Sītā—his best friend and his wife—is documented in many tales of heroism and epic poetry. He is a fitting guardian for the heart chakra and its loving emotions.

(*The Full Moon*)

Your heart chakra is also aligned with the full moon. This is the moon at its brightest and full of energy. The full moon illuminates the whole world, just like the love inside your heart chakra illuminates you. An open heart chakra is filled with love and brimming with purpose and passion. Like the moon, it has reached its zenith, its peak state. Unlike the moon, you can keep your heart chakra like this and prevent your love from waning.

ALL CHAKRAS HAVE a different color that represents their vibrational frequency. When combined together, they produce white light, symbolic of the whole person. The color associated with the heart chakra is green. This is a wonderfully hopeful color, one that is associated with nature, growth, and renewal. It also makes you feel calm, balanced, and gentle; all feelings synonymous with being loved.

HOW TO KNOW IF YOUR HEART CHAKRA NEEDS HELP

A happy heart chakra allows free-flowing energy that attracts all forms of love. If it is balanced, you are capable of loving yourself and making favorable decisions for yourself and your future. You won't feel like entering any conflict, and you will enjoy harmonizing with the world around you. You may also feel more forgiving and empathetic towards other people.

But, when your heart chakra is blocked or unbalanced, you can find it difficult to give and receive love, both from yourself and from those around you.

Signs that your heart chakra is blocked include:

- Withdrawing from the world and others. A blocked heart chakra can make you feel unworthy of love, so you shy away from friends and family, unwilling to accept the love that they offer you.
- Feelings of loneliness and depression. Being unable to love yourself can lead to feelings of worthlessness and an inability to see a future because you don't think that you deserve the happiness you see in others.
- Finding it difficult to maintain healthy relationships with friends, family, or partners. Sometimes this can be due to jealous behavior,

and other times you can become overly submissive, trying anything to please others.

- There are physical symptoms that can also be signs of an unbalanced heart chakra. These include:

- Pain in your shoulders, arms, hands, and upper back. It's easy to write this kind of pain off as an injury, muscle strain, or being caused by bad posture or high levels of stress. If typical treatments don't seem to have any effect, then it might be time to look for a more spiritual cure.

- Breathing issues such as asthma and shortness of breath. You might even find that your lung capacity appears to be reduced. A blocked heart chakra won't be able to energize these important organs, causing them to wither spiritually.

- Heart problems and problems with your circulation. You might experience palpitations, poor circulation to your fingers and toes, and find that your blood pressure is too high or too low. These are all clear signs that something is out of balance and your energy body isn't functioning properly.

Because the heart chakra embodies two major bodily systems—the circulatory system and the respiratory system—I'm going to divide the focus for the next section in two. The lungs and the heart have very different focuses and behaviors, and there are some heart chakra herbs that have more affinity for one than the other. It's important to know which is which, so you can find the most effective herbs for you.

HEART HEALING WITH NATURE

The first major organ associated with your heart chakra is the heart itself. Your heart controls the ebb and flow of love and is the center of your courage and self-belief. It is strong but also delicate and can be easily damaged by betrayal and grief.

THE CIRCULATORY SYSTEM: *Going With the Flow*

Just as your heart chakra lies at the center of your energy body, your heart is the center of your circulatory system. This is the network of vessels—also called the vascular system—which carry the blood around the body, bringing nourishment to your tissues and removing carbon dioxide. The blood leaves your heart and travels to your lungs, where it is enriched with oxygen before returning to your heart. Then it is pumped out again, this time going to your organs and muscles.

Your heart is made of four chambers, two on each side. The right side sends the blood to the lungs, and when it returns, it enters the chambers on the left side instead. The blood always flows in the same direction because these chambers have valves between them, and they shut off to prevent the blood from going the wrong way.

A healthy heart will pump blood effectively, while a healthy vascular system will make sure all the nutrients and oxygen it carries make it to their destinations. Using herbal tonics can help to ensure clear blood vessels and a strong heart with a regular rhythm. They will also nourish your spiritual heart, which is the center of your ability to love and be loved. A strong and open spiritual heart gives you the courage to share your feelings and speak up for your truth.

HEART INTELLIGENCE

We talk about making decisions with our heads or our hearts, but there's actually a lot of truth to that statement. Research has shown that 90% of the communication between your brain and your heart actually comes from the heart and not the other way around (scienceandnonduality, 2017). What this means is that changes in the rhythm of your heart are guiding your brain's response: if you're scared, your heartbeat will quicken, telling your brain to prepare your body's fight or flight response, not, as previously thought, is your brain telling your heart to beat faster.

Your heart rhythm also changes depending on who you are with. If you are with people you know and trust, your heart rhythm has less variation, but if you're in a room of strangers, it is more likely to be irregular. This just goes to show the incredible influence that our energy fields have over those around us. Our heart energy is particularly strong because it is powered by love, and when we feel that love from others, it has such a positive effect.

HEART HEALING WITH SPIRITUAL HERBALISM

Your heart can be damaged by disease and physical trauma, but it can also be damaged by emotional trauma, and these scars can be the hardest to heal. Commercial medicine won't heal a broken heart or help you rebuild after being emotionally let down by those around you. Recipes that are crafted by considering the ideas of spiritual herbalism are able to target both physical and emotional scars. The chemicals within the herbs themselves work to heal physical problems by doing things like strengthening the heart muscle, removing cholesterol and blockages in the blood vessels, and promoting high oxygen absorption. But the herbs also use their spiritual energy to work with your heart chakra, removing blockages that could be stunting the energy flow.

It's natural for your body to want to protect itself from harm, and your heart chakra will close itself off if it senses that something painful or traumatic is coming. This makes it harder to receive love and increases feelings of isolation and loneliness. Often your heart chakra will react based on past trauma, so if someone has hurt you before, it will preemptively close off around that person again, or if you find yourself in similar circumstances with someone new, your heart chakra will assume that they are going to act the same way. Overcoming this historical trauma and teaching your heart chakra that it's ok to be open can take a lot of work. Meditations, visualizations, and heart tonics will all support your heart chakra through the healing process.

Hawthorn (Crataegus Mongyna)

The hawthorn bush is a spiky tree with delicate white flowers that bloom in May—lending the tree its traditional British nickname of the May Tree. These blossoms turn into the recognizable deep red berries that are characteristic of the hawthorn. These berries are best harvested in late fall when they are fully ripe, but make sure you take care not to prick yourself on this herb's thorns. The thorns remind us that it is sometimes necessary to guard our hearts against those who may hurt us.

Hawthorn trees are native to England and much of Central Europe, as well as North Africa. They will also grow in the temperate regions of the United States. You can grow them from seeds, but trees grow slowly, so your best option is probably to purchase a healthy sapling. They love the sun, so make sure you plant your hawthorn where it can bask in the warm rays.

You can use hawthorn berries, flowers, and young leaves in recipes, as people have been doing for thousands of years.

Hawthorn has been traditionally used to strengthen the physical heart and act as an energizing and stimulating tonic. In addition to this, modern uses of hawthorn have shown it to act on the blood vessels as well, increasing blood flow, reducing the buildup of cholesterol, and regulating your blood pressure. What is wonderful about hawthorn is that it will adapt how it affects you, depending on your needs, e.g., It will raise low blood pressure or lower high blood pressure.

The constituents of hawthorn that have medicinal qualities are flavonoids, saponins, tannins, and antioxidants. Tannins work to prevent bacteria or other unwanted molecules from attaching to your body's cells. They are very effective at stopping cholesterol from building up in your blood vessels, thereby ensuring your circulatory system is free of blockages.

Spiritually, hawthorn is a hot herb that energizes and invigorates your energy. It corresponds to the planet Mars and connects to our primal desires, including the wants and passions of the heart. Hawthorn inspires courage; courage to open your heart after trauma, courage to love yourself, and courage to move on from the loss of love in your life. It is excellent for healing a broken heart because it brings renewed fire energy into your energy body and literally stokes the fires of your heart that can become cold and dampened with heartache. It can also be used as a general tonic to keep your heart chakra open.

Hawthorn is a very gentle herb with very few side effects or contraindications, meaning it is safe to be used by most people and over long periods of time. Anyone who is taking prescription heart medication or who suffers from ulcerating conditions should check with their doctor before taking hawthorn supplements.

ROSE (ROSA DAMASCENA)

You can't talk about herbs for the heart without mentioning the humble rose. These flowers have been associated with love and romance for thousands of years, dating back to the ancient Romans and Greeks. The plants themselves have been cultivated for 5,000 years, and there have been fossilized roses found that date back over 35 million years. Today they come in all different colors and are cultivated around the world, but it is the red varieties that are most often used for medicinal purposes. Roses are recognizable for their distinct perfume, the product of an essential oil secreted by both the petals and the leaves.

Roses aren't found so often in the wild now, but they are

easy to buy and just as easy to grow, just not from seed. You buy the plants either with bare roots or as small shrubs from nurseries. Best planted in the spring once the frosts have finished, you'll need to make sure you have well-drained soil and have chosen a position where the plants won't be scorched by the afternoon sun.

As with the hawthorn, the rose flower is protected by thorny stems—another reminder that our delicate hearts would benefit from protection if they are to remain open and giving. The rose, like love itself, is not just fragile and beautiful but also vibrant, healing, and strong. It is the perfect symbol for this vital emotion. It is the rose petals that are harvested and used today by both herbalists and the pharmaceutical industry, although if you forgo plucking the flowers, they will mature into rosehips, and they also contain marvelous healing properties.

Historically, rose has been used in love potions, as a perfume, and in herbalism to disguise the less agreeable flavors and odors of other herbs. It is still used today for the same reasons—although love potions are rarely commercially available—and it is also used in the beauty industry for its ability to tighten, hydrate, and refresh tired skin.

Rose petals are full of vitamins A, C, and E, as well as antioxidants and anti-inflammatory chemicals. They can be taken as a tonic to support heart function and keep your cholesterol numbers low. Rose also works as a hemostatic, interacting with your blood to increase clotting functions and counteract some of the symptoms of blood loss, like headache and a lack of energy. It is a cooling herb, as indicated by its anti-inflammatory nature, and rose water or rose tea is an effective treatment for overheating and fever.

Taking rose is also a wonderful way to relieve the stress and tension that comes from dealing with negative emotions. Whether you're angry, sad, or heartbroken, taking a rose tonic or diffusing rose essential oils will help to moderate and calm you, enabling your energy to return to a more neutral state. The essential oils in rose petals have a mild sedative quality that is exceptionally useful in these situations.

Rose is another extremely gentle herb and is most often used without side effects. It's always worth checking with your doctor before taking any supplements or tonics, just to make sure.

CAYENNE (CAPSICUM ANNUUM)

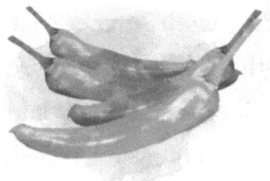

The humble chili pepper is more often found in the kitchen than the medicine cabinet, but it carries potent healing properties that will revitalize your heart and bring it back to life after emotional trauma.

This herb grows naturally in tropical climates; originally from Central America and the Caribbean, it is also cultivated in India and Europe. Many people choose to grow their own peppers as kitchen plants, and they thrive with a little care and attention. You can grow them from seeds or purchase the young plants already potted. Keep them warm, well-watered, and in full sunlight to ensure a good harvest. The fruits can be harvested in the summer once they have ripened from green to yellow or red.

The fruits can be cooked and eaten or dried and ground into a powder. You can also buy cayenne pepper powder in the grocery store or as capsules to be swallowed with water. The Mayans used to value the powder as a treatment for wounds and believed that rubbing the powder into cuts and wounds would burn away any disease and infection. They were absolutely right because cayenne has antimicrobial properties, meaning it kills off harmful bacteria that can go on to cause infections.

Cayenne is ruled by the planet Mars. This gives it great power and strength and makes it a great defender against serious conditions like cardiac arrest and strokes. The stimulating powers of cayenne are unrivaled, and it can quickly and effectively improve your circulation and your blood pressure. Cayenne also works to help your blood absorb more oxygen and nutrients, which it then delivers to your muscles and tissues. This, in turn, will increase your energy levels and bring the spring back to your step.

Unsurprisingly, cayenne is a hot herb with extreme heating properties. People with a hot constitution should avoid it or risk complications from overheating. Its hot nature comes from the chemical capsaicin, which is also responsible for cayenne's anti-inflammatory and pain-killing properties. Capsaicin stimulates your body's pain receptors, and doing this can help you to increase your pain tolerance and reduce your sensitivity. It also stimulates your digestive system and boosts your metabolism.

Because cayenne is such a powerful herb, its effects can be too strong for some people. It should not be used externally on sensitive skin because it can cause pain and a burning feeling. Although it can have many benefits for the digestive system, its heat can irritate existing conditions, so you should not take it if you suffer from ulcers, IBS, acid reflux, or any other form of digestive inflammation. If you take cayenne and find it is causing irritation, you can counter it with something cooling like milk, yogurt, or ice cream.

Motherwort (Leonurus Cardiaca)

This herb's Latin name literally means "Lionhearted," which will give you an indication of its benefits. Motherwort targets its support towards the heart and vascular system, but it is also a strong emotional herb, capable of healing heart trauma and adding layers of protection—this is another heart herb with thorns that will armor your heart against future heartbreak.

Motherwort is part of the mint family, but it grows in tall spires like a foxglove. These spires bloom with pretty pink flowers in midsummer and are punctuated by single leaves that stick out like the legs on a centipede: motherwort has a very distinctive appearance and looks great at the back of any garden borders. It is native to the UK and mainland Europe, where it grows as a wild weed. Like most weeds, it isn't particular about its growing conditions and will thrive in both full shade and full sunlight.

The entire herb is used to make medicine, so harvest the plant just above the ground and hang them in bunches to dry. Shred the leaves and flowers from the stems and store them in a dry container until needed. Unlike other mints, motherwort has a very bitter flavor, meaning that it doesn't taste great if brewed as a tea unless you combine it with more palatable flavors.

Because motherwort is a cooling, bitter herb, it also falls into the category of drying herbs. This makes it an excellent tonic for removing excess heat and moisture from the body. Heartburn and indigestion will be soothed by motherwort, and it's also worth taking if you suffer from conditions that leave fluid in the lungs, like pneumonia.

For a long time, motherwort has been used as a tonic for heart palpitations, nervous conditions, and fainting. It is known as a cardiac strengthener and a nervine—an herb that targets and supports the nervous system. The combination of these two qualities means it works wonders to combat signs and symptoms of stress like high blood pressure, irregular heart rate, and the feeling of having butterflies in your stomach.

The active ingredients of motherwort include flavonoids, alkaloids, and iridoids. Alkaloids are often used to treat cardiac problems, and these antioxidants are great for protecting the heart from damage, both physical and emotional. Motherwort is also known as an emmenagogue, which means it stimulates and encourages blood flow. This can help to regulate the female reproductive system and encourage menstruation in cases of amenorrhea. For this reason, people prone to bleeding disorders and people who are pregnant should avoid taking motherwort.

Because of its ability to affect the female reproductive system, motherwort is aligned with the planet Venus. Venus is also the planet that rules over love, tying motherwort even more strongly to the heart chakra. Finally, Venus and motherwort both exert their influence in a soft, gentle manner, making this an ideal herb to restore your emotional and spiritual balance without having to tolerate a lot of side effects.

RECIPES AND RELAXATION

Heart Happiness Boosting Syrup

Syrups are sweet medicines made by reducing decoctions and adding something sugary for taste. The last thing you want when dealing with a broken heart is to have to swallow something bitter, so cheer up your tastebuds as well as your heart with this sweet restorative. The following recipe makes about a liter, and you can store it in the refrigerator for up to 45 days.

You will need:

- 2 tbsps of rose hips, dried
- 2 tbsps of hawthorn berries, dried
- 2 tbsps of raspberries, dried
- 1 tbsp of ginger root, dried
- 1 cup of brandy

- 1 cup of honey, organic if possible
- 1 tbsp of rosewater

Simmer 4 cups of water on the stove. Add the dried herbs and leave for half an hour. When you have extracted the goodness from the herbs, strain the resulting decoction through a fine mesh. Gently stir in the honey, continuing to agitate the mixture until the honey has completely blended with the water. Repeat with the brandy and the rosewater. Decant your syrup into a glass jar to store. Take one tablespoon up to three times a day as needed.

THE WAY to Your Heart Chakra Truffles

Chocolates have a long-standing association with love and often symbolize the giving of affection. Cacao is also a great heart herb with antioxidant properties—what more excuse do you need for a little indulgence? There's no set dosage for these; feel free to snack on them whenever you need a little love pick me up.

You will need:

- ⅔ of a cup of cacao powder (or cocoa powder, although this is less beneficial)
- ¼ of a cup of cacao butter

- 1 tbsp of hawthorn berries, powdered
- ½ tsp of cinnamon
- ½ tsp of ginger powder
- 1 tsp of rose petals, powdered
- a pinch of cayenne powder
- 2-3 tbsp of honey, raw

First, you'll need to melt the cacao butter in a heat-proof bowl. Over a pot of water on the stove is preferable, but if you want to use a microwave, just be careful not to let it burn. Stir the rest of the ingredients into the melted butter, keeping back ⅓ of the cacao powder to coat the truffles.

Leave the mixture to chill in the refrigerator until firm. Using a teaspoon, scoop out a walnut-sized amount, and roll it in the remaining cacao powder until you have a coated ball of chocolatey goodness. Keep your truffles in an airtight container in the refrigerator and eat as needed.

LOVE YOURSELF SMOOTHIE

Smoothies have become a really popular way to get your daily fruit and veg, and they're also great after a workout or as a breakfast drink. This one is super simple and packed full of juicy, antioxidant fruits that will show your body some love. It's a bright and vibrant green designed to invigorate your heart chakra.

You will need:

- 2 green apples, peeled and cored.
- ½ cup of pineapple, fresh or tinned
- ½ a cup of mango, frozen
- 1 cup of baby kale

Blitz all the ingredients in your blender or smoothie maker, adding a little extra water or apple juice if you like your smoothie to have a thinner texture. If you don't have frozen mango, you can use fresh pieces, but add some ice chips to thicken it.

HEART HEALING MEDITATION

Your heart is such an important organ that it deserves a special meditation that focuses on recharging and opening its capacity for love. Because it is associated with the heart chakra, we can use a lot of chakral influences to help stimulate and strengthen it. Your heart chakra is associated with the sense of touch, so we're going to combine a gentle massage with this meditation to help to recharge your energy. If you have some crystals, you can use these in the massage; good crystals for the heart chakra include rose quartz, jade, emerald, aventurine, and covellite. You could also infuse your calm space with some rosewater or rose essential oils.

- Settle yourself in a comfortable seated position with your shoulders back and your chest open. Breathe in, slowly and deeply, for a count of four. Feel your lungs expanding in your chest, filling you with oxygen. Breathe out sharply, imagining the air from your lungs rushing to your organs. Be conscious of your diaphragm while you are breathing - it should expand so that your lungs can fill your whole chest. Place your hands on your diaphragm and feel it moving. Repeat for 10 breaths.

- Move your hands from your diaphragm to the center of your breastbone. If you have crystals, hold them between your fingers and touch them to your skin; otherwise, use the tips of your fingers. Massage up and outward from your breastbone in small circles, breathing in as you go. Breathe out as your fingers return to the center. Close your eyes and imagine you are drawing these circles around the edge of a bright green circle that is getting brighter with each breath you take. When you are ready, take one final deep breath in, and on the breath out, imagine that green light leaving your heart chakra and traveling into the world, touching everything you love.

- Look down inside yourself and imagine you are now left with a small pink light in the center of your chest. That is the love you have saved for yourself. See it grow bright and strong, symbolizing your strength of character, your courage, and your worthiness. Finish with five more breaths, chanting the syllable *yam* on each exhalation. Slowly open your eyes and take in the love and beauty of the world around you.

HEALING YOUR LUNGS WITH NATURE

The second major organs associated with your heart chakra are the lungs. Your heart is ruled by the sun, but your lungs correspond to the planet Mercury. This planet deals with information and your nervous system, and these qualities converge in the lungs as a particular emotion: grief. Fresh grief is painful and dynamic, producing tears and howls of anguish. This is processed in the heart, where it is felt deeply and eventually overcome. The lungs deal with unresolved grief, the eternal feeling of there being something missing. This is the grief that drains your emotions, leaving you feeling sluggish and disconnected from reality.

Grief can linger in the lungs for years, and you might be completely unaware of it. Sometimes we carry with us feelings of grief from our childhood that we never completely dealt with because we were so young and unable to understand. Other times, the grief we are burdened with is ancestral, stemming from generations of hurt, persecution, secrets, and lies.

HOW RETAINED GRIEF CAN AFFECT YOUR WELLBEING

Storing grief over a long period of time can be damaging and draining for your lungs. It weighs them down and saps their energy, creating blockages in the flow around your energy body. With your lungs in a weakened emotional state, they are more susceptible to physical problems. This includes diseases of the lung such as pneumonia, bronchitis, colds, and chest infections. It might even be the reason why one could find it difficult to give up smoking, as weakened energy often leads to addictive tendencies.

When we talk about grief, we often focus on the idea of sadness and loss, but grief can also come out of anger. If you've recently had a disagreement or an angry exchange with someone, you could be holding on to grief from that argument. This negative emotion can drain energy from your immune system, inviting cold viruses to take up residence. Often, resolving this grief can clear away the sniffles faster than over-the-counter medication.

LUNG HEALING WITH SPIRITUAL HERBALISM

While both the heart and lungs are governed by your heart chakra, they behave in completely different ways and respond to herbs with different qualities. Where the heart loves warming herbs (although not exclusively), the lungs respond better to cooling and moist herbs that repair the delicate mucous membranes within. The following herbs have been used for thousands of years to treat lung diseases or as a tonic to promote lung health.

MULLEIN (VERBASCUM THAPSUS)

Mullein is another wonderful wild plant that is found in Europe, Asia, and the northern parts of Africa, as well as the United States. It's a hedgerow plant and tends to pop up in fields that have been given back to nature, as well as along roadsides, abandoned buildings, and anywhere humans haven't begun to interfere. This distinctive herb can grow to five feet in height and is crowned by a spear of yellow flowers. Its leaves are long and broad at the base of the stalk, tapering to a more slender shape, and the color becomes a lighter green at the top.

The leaves and the flowers are used medicinally, either fresh or dried. You can extract mullein oil from both, and this makes an effective salve for eczema and other skin irritations. Mullein also contains saponins, flavonoids, iridoids, and polyphenols—cramming a lot of anti-inflammatory and antioxidant properties into one herb.

You should be able to find mullein growing wild, and if you find one plant, you'll find hundreds because they spread their seeds far and wide. Because it is used to toughing it in the wild, mullein is easy to grow and requires little care. Sow the seeds outdoors in the fall, as they need the cold of winter to kickstart their growth. The plants will thrive in either full or partial sunlight and in all different soils.

The ancient Greeks used mullein to treat coughs and congested lungs more than two thousand years ago. Mullein has such a strong effect on the lungs that it was even used to treat tuberculosis and asthma before the pharmaceutical methods we use today came into common use. Nowadays, mullein is used primarily for its mucilage, a thick and gooey jelly-like substance that is great at calming inflammation and reducing irritation, especially in lung tissue.

Mullein is a cooling herb with moist energy that gives it a natural affinity with the lungs. Your lungs can't absorb oxygen effectively if they are dry, so their tissue must stay moist and coated in a thin layer of mucus. When they get inflamed or irritated, this can raise the temperature and cause this moisture to dry up, so treatment with moist, cooling herbs is a must.

Another superpower of mullein is that it works as an expectorant, helping to move blockages of heavy mucus that can accumulate when you have a cold or if toxins like cigarette smoke have been introduced into your lungs. Expectorants unstick this mucus and help you to cough it up, ridding your body of physical contaminants but also helping to expel emotional contaminants as well.

Even though mullein has cooling energy, it is associated with the fire element. In fact, dried mullein leaves have been used to make candle wicks and bring light to the darkness for centuries. Its planetary correspondence is with Mercury and Saturn, signifying its dual roles as treatments for both the respiratory system and the skin.

Mullein is a gentle herb with few side effects or contraindications. There have not been many studies on its effects during pregnancy and while breastfeeding, so it should be avoided in these situations. Sometimes mullein oil applied externally can cause a skin irritation called contact dermatitis, so it's a good idea to patch test before using, especially if you have sensitive skin.

Eucalyptus (Eucalyptus Globulus)

This herb is native to the island of Tasmania, but it has been introduced to the Mediterranean and other subtropical regions, where it is grown in plantations. It is a staple herb of Aboriginal herbalism, where it was used topically to help wounds heal. It has also been adopted into Ayurvedic medicine and traditional Chinese medicine, where it has been recognized for its antiseptic and antimicrobial properties.

Although some forms of eucalyptus trees don't grow much taller than a shrub, this form can grow as tall as 230 ft. It has a distinctive blue outer bark that hides a softer, cream bark underneath. Eucalyptus tree leaves can be 12 in. long, and they are a shiny, dark green with a waxy texture. In the summer, the trees erupt in a spray of white flowers with distinctive, spiky petals that make them look like sea anemones. They are loved by bees and insects alike, which can make them a great addition to an environmentally conscious garden.

If you do want to grow eucalyptus at home, it's best to opt for a shrub version unless you have a sizable growing area. Plant them somewhere sunny and make sure the soil isn't too boggy. Their leaves droop down like a willow tree, giving them their distinctive appearance, and can be pruned to restrict growth if needed.

Eucalyptus has a warming quality that helps it to reduce and stabilize inflammations. Its affinity with the respiratory system aligns it with the planet Mercury. Nowadays, it is commonly used as a decongestant to clear blocked noses and soothe a sore throat. Eucalyptus is another expectorant, helping to bring up mucus and remove toxins from the lungs.

The active constituents of eucalyptus that make it a great healing herb are flavonoids, tannins, and essential oils called cineol and pinene, the latter of which carries anti-inflammatory and antioxidant properties. These essential oils are extracted from the leaves of the eucalyptus tree and are used in modern medicine to clear mucus from the nasal passages, throat, and lungs. Breathing in a eucalyptus steam bath gives you almost instant relief from blocked sinuses and will start to break up the mucus that can gather in your lungs during a chest infection. You must not ingest eucalyptus oil, but you can brew a delicious cup of tea from the dried leaves.

Dried eucalyptus leaves are safe to use, even by children. In fact, eucalyptus is an ingredient often found in children's chest rubs, essential oil plug-ins, and soothing bath oils. The essential oil, however, can be toxic in large quantities or if used for a prolonged period of time. It must never be used internally or on children.

Elecampane (Inula Helenium)

Elecampane is an herb of British origin that has been transported around the world for cultivation and is now found also growing wild throughout the rest of Europe and the temperate areas of Asia and North America. It prefers to grow in wild pastures and open fields, by the side of the road, and at the base of cliffs and mountains. Elecampane thrives in moist soil and shady areas where it can grow undisturbed.

Suppose you wanted to plant it in your garden; elecampane would thrive at the back of a herbaceous border with other wildflowers. The plants can grow to 5ft in height and have stalks that rise up from a base of long, thin green leaves. In the summer, these stalks are topped with a spray of daisy-like heads with large yellow centers and long, thin, yellow petals. They are very distinctive and attractive, bringing a sunny quality to any garden.

The plants are harvested for their roots, which are harvested from plants that are around two years old. Elecampane roots contain inulin, a starchy prebiotic that has a lot of benefits for digestive health. It also works deeply within the lungs by adding a protective coat to the bronchial tubes and has been used effectively for hundreds of years as a treatment for diseases from common coughs and colds to tuberculosis. Other important medicinal constituents of elecampane include mucilage, saponins, alkaloids, and essential oils.

Elecampane is also an emotionally healing herb. It attaches itself to buried and stagnant grief and brings it to the surface, ready to be expelled. It has warming and dry energies, which break down old mucus membranes and encourage new layers to grow to replace them. This stimulates the renewal of the lung tissue and affects a positive change by creating movement. Ruled by Saturn, elecampane is a truly universal herb, proving to be a wonderful tonic not only for the lungs but also for the digestive system, uterus, and soft tissues.

This herb is not to be taken by anyone who is pregnant or breastfeeding. If you are taking any kind of prescription medication for an existing condition, you should always talk to your doctor before taking any herbs, including elecampane. Do not take more than the recommended dose, as it can cause diarrhea and sickness in large quantities.

RECIPES AND MEDITATIONS TO RELEASE GRIEF

Decongestant Syrup

This formula is an effective treatment for congestion in the lungs that you just can't seem to shift. It combines several herbal expectorants to get the mucus moving, but they will also work to dislodge buried grief, so you can cleanse yourself physically and emotionally all at once. The herbs are listed as parts, so you can make up a large jar of mixed herbs, ready to brew fresh teas, tinctures, and syrups as needed.

You will need:

- 2 parts licorice root
- 1 part elecampane
- 1 part echinacea
- 1 part cinnamon
- 1 part marshmallow
- ¼ part ginger

Thoroughly combine the dried herbs and store in an airtight container until needed. To brew the syrup, add 2 oz of your mixture to a pot and top up with 1 quart of cold water. Simmer over low heat until the liquid has reduced down to 1 pint, then strain the herbs and return the liquid to the heat. Add 1 cup of honey and stir until thoroughly blended. If you want, you can also add a tablespoon of brandy. Remove from the heat and allow to cool before pouring into a glass bottle or jar. Store in the refrigerator. Take 1 teaspoon as needed, up to three times a day.

RESPIRATORY REPAIR TEA

In order for your respiratory tracts and lungs to be in top condition, they need to be kept moist. This is achieved by a thin layer of helpful mucus that coats all the tubes. However, this can dry up when there is inflammation or congestion full of foreign bodies, like viruses, bacteria, and cigarette smoke. This tea is a great way to encourage your body to replenish this mucus membrane, as well as clear out some of the old, ineffective mucus.

You will need:

- 1 ½ tsp of mullein herb, dried
- 1 tsp of eucalyptus leaves, dried
- 1 tsp of marshmallow root, dried
- Honey to sweeten

Boil 1/2 liter of water on the stove, add the dried herbs, and keep boiling for 10 minutes. Strain the tea into a mug and add honey to taste. You can use other sweeteners if you prefer, but honey is great because it also has a soothing quality for sore throats, so if you're feeling a little under the weather, it's an added bonus.

RELEASING GRIEF THROUGH SOUND HEALING

Your lungs are naturally built for release, but sometimes they need a little help to clear themselves. While removing carbon dioxide is easy, your lungs should also be able to use your exhalations to remove negative energy, retained grief, and exhausted emotions. One way to do this is through sound healing.

- Stand in your neutral position with your feet firmly planted on the ground. Raise your arms above your shoulders, with your elbows bent so that the tips of your fingers are by your ears. Push your elbows back so that they pull your shoulders and fully open your chest. Tilt your head slightly back to straighten your throat.
- In this position, take a deep breath, feeling it fill every part of your lungs. As you exhale, make a long hissing sound and visualize your breath pulling all the grief and negativity out of your lungs. Imagine this polluted breath as a dark gray color and watch it leave your body and float away.

- Now, move your hands down to your chest and place one over each lung. Take a series of deep breaths through your nose, this time visualizing clean, white energy filling your lungs, getting into all the air sacs and all the grooves of the tissue.

You can repeat this exercise as often as you need to help your lungs to empty their stores of grief. If grief is deep-seated, it will take more than one cycle of breaths to get it moving, let alone remove it all, so you may want to perform this ritual often.

5

THE THROAT CHAKRA

This is the fifth of the chakras, counting upward from your root chakra at the base of your spine. The throat chakra—also called Vishuddha—is found exactly where you would expect it to be: in your throat. More specifically, it is located at the point where your throat meets the center of your collarbones. It governs your skills of communication, both verbal and nonverbal. As part of this, your throat chakra is also the center of your inspiration and creative expression.

THROAT CHAKRA ASSOCIATIONS

Your throat chakra is the link between your heart and your brain. Both have their own sense of intuition that guide their decision-making process, but they don't always necessarily agree. The throat chakra is the balancing point between the two, weighing up the pros and cons of both head and heart and finally allowing you to speak your truth. The truth is a powerful thing to wield, and we must use it wisely and carefully to stand up for ourselves, our beliefs, and those who need our help. A strong, stable throat chakra will give you the power to do this.

Expressing your truth also involves self-expression, and the ways in which you let the world know who you are are all rooted in the throat chakra. This is the center of your internal energy and the manifestation of your personality and individuality. It is also the center for your creative expression and how you communicate your art to the world.

Effective communication requires a balance between speaking and listening, and your throat chakra governs both your throat and your ears. If your chakra is unbalanced, then you won't pay equal attention to both sides of the conversation, which will drastically affect your ability to communicate with others and with the world around you.

If your throat chakra is well-balanced and allows your life energy to flow smoothly, you will find speaking to others or to an audience comfortable and easy. Communicating your needs, opinions, and ideas will elicit positive responses from others, and they will enjoy listening to you because your speech is pleasant and well-constructed.

WHAT INFLUENCES THE THROAT CHAKRA?

The throat chakra is associated with the element of ether or space, otherwise known as Akhasa. In the West, we are used to only four elements—earth, water, fire, and air—but Eastern disciplines tell of a fifth element that covers more ethereal concerns. Ether is the fabric of the soul and the purest element: which is why the throat chakra is given the name of Vishuddha, which means "purity."

The throat chakra is also influenced by Mercury, the planet of communication. Mercury doesn't just enable verbal communication; it governs how our bodies and brains listen to what the universe is telling us through our five senses and our intuition. Communicating the sights, sounds, smells, tastes, and sensations of your world all fall to your throat chakra, and if its energy is out of balance, you might feel like you are out of step with reality.

All the chakras have a Hindu deity that watches over them, and for the throat chakra, this is Sadashiva. Sadashiva is one of the forms of Shiva, the god of destruction. In this form, Sadashiva has five faces that represent the forces of the universe. Five is an important number here, as the throat chakra embodies the fifth element, the five senses, and is the fifth chakra.

Just like the heart chakra, the throat chakra is also aligned with the full moon. This is a time to fully embrace who you are and what you bring to the world. If you are a creative type, for example, a singer, writer, or painter, you should take advantage of the full moon to begin a new project or clear out any cobwebs and creative blocks that have been hampering your work. During the full moon, your creativity and powers of communication will be at their peak, so make sure you take full advantage.

Another way to tap into your throat chakra is by channeling the color blue. The shade itself doesn't matter, but try to stick with true blues rather than tending towards a green-blue mix like turquoise. Blue is a relaxing color that promotes calm, but it also has ties to healing and communication. In color therapy, blue hues are used to encourage patients to open up about their feelings and true desires—something that sounds very much in the throat chakra's wheelhouse.

HOW TO KNOW IF YOUR THROAT CHAKRA NEEDS HELP

A blocked throat chakra won't stop you from communicating completely—although suddenly losing your voice can be a sign that your energies are out of balance—but it will mean that you find it harder to find yourself heard and understood.

Some of the signs of an unbalanced throat chakra include:

- Feeling shy and uncomfortable around other people. You might worry about what they think of you or be concerned that you won't fit in.

- An increased sensitivity to loud noises. This can mean both sudden noises, like fireworks or sirens, and general high noise levels that you would find in a bar, busy restaurant, or at a ballgame.

- A difficulty expressing or recognizing tone. Speakers with a deficient throat chakra often speak in a single, droning monotone, with little to no inflection. They can also find it difficult to sing in key, as deviating from their usual pitch doesn't feel natural.

- Being whiny, underhanded, and manipulative. Here, communication is centered around guilting or persuading others to do things rather than listening to their wants and needs. Complaining if they don't get their way is another sign to watch out for in people with underactive throat chakras.

- Constantly talking over other people, having to have the last word, and dismissing the opinions of others. Having a conversation with someone like this is akin to being run over by a slow-moving train that goes on, and on, without any consideration for your interest or well-being.

- Suffering from writer's block or feeling that your inspiration has up and left you. Excess throat chakra energy is blocking you from hearing the conversation of the universe and finding your muse.

- Unbalanced chakras can have physical symptoms as well. You will find that body parts that have an affinity with this chakra—your throat, nose, ears, shoulders, neck, and thyroid gland—start to show signs of unhappiness.
- Physical indications of an unbalanced chakra could include:
- Having an over or underactive thyroid gland. This can lead to hormonal imbalances, weight gain, and low energy levels.
- Recurring mouth and teeth problems, such as bleeding gums and being prone to cavities.
- Finding it easy to pick up colds and sore throats. Viruses and bacteria can take root in your throat and sinuses when your energy flow is weakened. If it seems like you're always sniffling and sneezing, try targeting your throat chakra with some healing herbal teas.
- Stiff neck and shoulder muscles. Your throat chakra works like the valve connecting your head and heart. If it cannot open and release the energy and emotions from each, they will build up and start to affect the area around this chakra.

USING HERBS TO UNBLOCK YOUR THROAT CHAKRA

When working with your throat chakra, one must give consideration to the chakras and bodily systems below it. Your throat is a passageway between your lungs and your stomach, bringing nourishment in and expelling waste chemicals. Any blockages, stagnant energy, or withheld emotions that are festering below will send negative energy through your throat. Herbs that work on your digestive system, like fennel, chamomile, and dandelion, will all also benefit your throat chakra.

Similarly, herbs that have an affinity with your lungs will use their anti-inflammatory and soothing qualities on your throat, which shares the same type of tissue and the same mucosal coating. It is necessary to employ the throat when removing mucus blockages and stagnant grief from your lungs, so be aware that its energy will be dampened by the passage of other negative energies. A good throat tonic that will keep your chakra in balance is vital to counteract these experiences.

THROAT CHAKRA HEALING WITH NATURE

Throat-beneficial herbs tend to be cleansing in nature because the throat can become clogged with debris, as well as being an easy target for viruses and bacteria. Remember that the herbs will work best when you use a whole spectrum supplement, dried herbs, or even grow your own.

Having your own supply of herbs in your garden or growing in the kitchen will really strengthen your relationship with their plant spirits and ensure that they are always working in your best interests.

You will find that many of the herbs listed to help your heart chakra—particularly those that have an affinity with the lungs—will also be beneficial for your throat chakra. This is because the lining of your mouth, throat, and lungs are made of the same mucus-lined tissue. Feel free to use them interchangeably or combine them in recipes for a soothing cup of tea.

A WARNING About Slippery Elm

Slippery elm is a type of elm tree that is native to North America and has been highly prized by Native American herbalists for centuries because of its soft, inner bark. This bark acts as a powerful demulcent—an herb that treats inflammation and restores the delicate mucus membranes that coat the mouth, throat, and lung tissue.

Slippery elm is highly effective, but this has led to problems with overharvesting. Even commercially bought slippery elm is most likely wildcrafted because the prevalence of elm diseases, such as Dutch Elm disease, makes it difficult and unprofitable to attempt cultivation. Basically, elm diseases spread so easily that they will wipe out entire plantations before the trees have reached maturity.

Because the medicinally useful part of the herb comes from the inner bark, it is only reached by stripping the outer bark, a process that the tree is unlikely to survive. While sustainable providers will harvest sparingly and from naturally felled specimens, the demand for slippery elm bark is so high that it has created a new type of criminal; the slippery elm poacher.

As responsible spiritual herbalists, we should not be using slippery elm as a herb until more sustainable farming practices become the norm. I actively urge you to use alternatives that are more ethically sourced, including marshmallow root and mullein leaves, both of which I have included in detail in this book.

Sage (Salvia Officinalis)

Good old sage is often a kitchen staple (and a staple in energetic and spiritual cleansing), but many people forget about its wonderful healing properties pertaining to the physical body. Its Latin name literally translates as "salvation used in medicine," and it was used medicinally by the Ancient Greeks, Romans, and Egyptians thousands of years ago. There are almost 1000 different types of sage plants, which are, in turn, also part of the family of mint plants, but only a few of them are edible or possess healing powers. The common sage that you find in the grocery store is the best for both cooking and well-being. This variety is native to Europe, especially the region around the Mediterranean, but there are other varieties—like white sage—which are native to the United States and are used in Native American herbalism.

Common sage is a bushy shrub that tends to grow no more than 2 ft tall. Its dusty green leaves are velvety and covered with tiny dimples, almost like the skin of a reptile.

In the summer months, the shrubs flower with tiny purple blooms that grow on stalks, separate from the leaves. It is a favorite plant of bees and insects and makes a wonderful addition to any garden. Sage is also extremely tolerant of harsh conditions and will grow whatever the temperature and in full sun or shade.

You can use the whole plant (except the root) for healing. Cut bunches of sage and hang them up to dry, or take fresh leaves and flowers as needed. The leaves contain a volatile oil that has many antiseptic, antioxidant, and anti-inflammatory properties. Sage is under the influence of Jupiter, which explains its wide variety of uses. Jupiter herbs bring vitality and joy, and many are adaptogenic, meaning they are incredibly intuitive and will automatically target specific problem areas.

It might actually be quicker to list the conditions that sage cannot help with because it is such a powerful and useful adaptogenic herb that it just brings healing energy whenever it is used. Sage has astringent and antibacterial qualities that make it an excellent, soothing treatment for sore throats, coughs, chest infections, and the other symptoms of colds and flu. It is a drying and cooling herb, which helps to counteract fevers and inflammation, as well as promotes the healing of burns when applied topically.

Sage is also an excellent herb to counter menopausal symptoms and painful periods. Its drying action works to decrease retained fluid that can lead to bloating and to reduce blood loss during menstruation. It can also be used to dry up breastmilk if it is no longer needed. Spiritually, sage is a powerful cleanser. It is used in smudging rituals to clear houses of negative energy and unwanted spirits, and it can do the same to your body by removing unwanted emotions and misplaced energy. In your throat chakra, this means clearing the way, so you can continue to express yourself as fully as possible.

Because of its strong drying effect, sage should not be taken during pregnancy or while breastfeeding—unless the aim is to reduce your milk supply. It is also not recommended for people who have recurring seizures. The above applies to a medicinal dose—you can still use sage to flavor your cooking.

ELDERFLOWER (SAMBUCUS CANADENSIS or Sambucus Nigra)

There is more than one variety of elder tree, and these two are very similar. The variety *canadensis* is native to Central and North America, while the *nigra* can be found in the wild all over Europe. Classified as either a large shrub or a small tree, it gives us elderflowers and elderberries, both of which have medicinal uses that have been honed over hundreds of years. The elder can grow up to 12 ft tall and has distinctive toothed leaves that are a rich, dark green on the top but lighter underneath.

The elderflowers themselves are a creamy color and grow as umbels: tiny flowers that are grouped together on the top of a stalk, a bit like an umbrella, with many umbels branching from the same main stalk. They appear in late spring and early summer, and they mature into elderberries in the fall. This is an easy herb to wildcraft because of the abundance of wild trees in their native habitats. When harvesting flowers, you should be mindful not to take them all so that others can also enjoy them and the resulting elderberry crops.

The European elder tree was once revered among Celtic and pagan cultures, who believed that old spirits would move into the trees and make them their homes. They would leave food and drinks as gifts for the tree spirits, and they were always asked for permission before cutting branches. Modern spiritual herbalism harks back to these early ideas, but it's no longer just elder trees that are considered to house plant spirits. Even further back, elderflowers were being used by the Ancient Egyptians to cool and soothe skin problems such as rashes and sunburns, but also to reduce wrinkles.

Elder trees are fantastic for herbalists because you can use flowers, berries, leaves, and bark to treat different complaints. Only the flowers and berries are eaten, as long as they have been dried or cooked first, because they both contain a chemical that can release small amounts of cyanide poison if eaten raw. The flowers themselves are mainly used for their volatile oil, vitamin C, tannins, and mucilage.

These dainty flowers have dry and cooling energies, which is what makes them a great remedy for colds and blocked sinuses: They can dry up the excess mucus that causes blockages and irritation without overheating and damaging the lining of your nose and throat. Their cooling properties can help you to restore or maintain your body's optimum temperature, either on a hot day or if you're suffering from a fever.

Elderflowers can lower your blood sugar, so they shouldn't be taken by anyone who is suffering from diabetes or other low blood sugar conditions or if you are about to have surgery. There is not a lot of research into the effects of elderflower during pregnancy, and while breastfeeding, so it is best to avoid it in these circumstances. If you take too much elderflower, you should seek medical advice straight away.

MARSHMALLOW ROOT (ALTHAEA *Officinalis*)

Although it conjures images of giant fluffy marshmallows growing on trees, the only thing growing from this delicious-sounding plant are pink and white flowers. Reaching a maximum of 5 ft tall, its leaves are shaped like hearts and covered with a soft down on both sides. This plant originated from Asia but now grows happily all over the world, much like its cousin, the common mallow (*malva neglecta*), and thrives when well-cared for in a garden.

The flowers, leaves, and roots are all harvested for medicinal purposes. You can harvest the flowers and leaves in early fall and hang them in bunches to dry. The roots are best harvested from a plant that is two or three years old: this allows for good growth of rootstock. Dig them up in the fall, chop them into pieces while still fresh, and then dry the roots in sections.

Marshmallow is a cooling and moistening herb, which makes it perfectly in harmony with the environment of your respiratory system, mouth, and throat. It is a demulcent, an emollient, and an effective expectorant; three qualities that show its effectiveness at treating imbalances, diseases, and infections that occur around your throat and throat chakra. Marshmallow corresponds with the moon and Venus, two gentle planetary energies that are attuned to your feminine energy and your intuition. The moon's primary influence is over your gut and the effective removal of waste, but this also aligns with your throat chakra, as it is the passageway by which waste is eliminated from your lungs.

Traditional marshmallow recipes come from all over the world. In China, marshmallow root is used as a treatment for hot flashes and night sweating, while in areas of the Middle East, it was used in cooking as a substitute for expensive foodstuffs. Arab herbalists used the leaves as a topical treatment for skin irritations and rashes.

Today, marshmallow is recognized for its wonderful soothing and healing properties. It is rich in the chemical mucilage, which, as previously mentioned, repairs the mucosal lining of your throat and lungs. Marshmallow root can be used as an effective treatment for coughs, sore throats, and recurring mouth ulcers. It is also an effective tonic to maintain the respiratory system and provide daily protection against airborne particles like pollution, smoke, and pollen. It is commonly taken as a supplement or brewed as marshmallow root tea.

Marshmallow root can cause some unwanted interactions with prescription medications, so you should always consult with your doctor before taking it. Because of its demulcent qualities, it can interfere with the absorption of medication through the stomach lining, so your dosage may no longer be correct. Do not adjust your own dosages! Known issues also occur with lithium and diabetes medication, as marshmallow works in the same way, increasing the effect.

Red Clover (Trifolium Pratense)

Red clover is an abundant herbal wildflower that can be found in meadows, pastures, woodland, by the roadside, and even growing on mountains. Originally found throughout Europe and Asia, it was brought to North America by settlers and let loose on the land. It has small, green, trifoliate leaves, which means they are grouped together in threes, and from these rise slender stems with flower heads on top. The red clover flower heads are made up of many thin reddish-purple petals that form a pine cone shape. It is the flowers that are harvested for their medicinal benefits.

Unfortunately, red clover is looked upon as a weed,

which unfairly gives it a bad reputation; it's actually an incredibly beneficial and useful plant to have in your garden. It grows long, deep roots, which help to anchor the soil and prevent erosion. It's also a favorite of bees because its flowers are full of nectar and pollen. Plant it as part of a wildflower section where it can grow tall, or use it as a grass substitute for an ornamental path—red clover is so hardy it doesn't mind being stepped on and mown short.

Traditional uses for red clover include treatments for relieving fever, clearing up colds, repairing tissue affected by lung diseases like bronchitis and tuberculosis, as well as external applications to soothe skin irritations. It was even once prescribed as a treatment for asthma. Red clover has a cooling energy, hence its affinity with the mouth and throat. Its active constituents include flavonoids, polysaccharides, and isoflavones—a type of phytoestrogen that has a similar effect on your body to its own estrogen.

One of the fantastic qualities red clover has is that it works as an alternative, meaning it helps the body to return to a normal state. It does this by removing waste products and purifying the bloodstream. It is also antispasmodic and an expectorant, making it yet another excellent herb for cleaning out the lungs, both of clogged mucus and negative energy. Red clover is often combined with herbs rich in mucilage, like mullein and elecampane, for the double effect of clearing the lungs and throat and then recoating their walls with a fresh mucosal lining.

You shouldn't take red clover if you are already on blood thinning medications because it can increase their effectiveness. Because of the phytoestrogens in red clover, it can reduce the effectiveness of hormonal birth control and should also be avoided by anyone who is pregnant or breast-feeding.

RECIPES AND RELAXATION

Superhoney

Honey has its own wonderful antibacterial properties for promoting healing and soothing inflammation, and when combined with this cocktail of herbs, you should have a powerful medicine to stop any cold or flu virus in its tracks. You can help yourself to a teaspoon of the finished product whenever you feel a tickle start in your throat, or stir it into an herbal tea for a warm, sweet, antimicrobial treat! You'll need a crockpot and some mason jars for this recipe, but it will keep in the cupboard for ages, so it's worth brewing up a big batch.

You will need:

- 1 cup of rosemary, fresh
- 1 cup of ginger root, fresh
- 1 cup of sage, fresh
- ½ a cup of thyme, fresh
- 3 cups of honey, organic if possible

Start by crushing your herbs to release their essential oils. You can do this with a pestle and mortar or with the end of a rolling pin and a bowl—just don't blitz in a blender. Fill a couple of mason jars with the herbs, distributing them as evenly as possible. Pour over the honey until the herbs are fully covered. Feel free to stir and top up if needed.

Pop the open jars into the crockpot and add water about ½ to ⅔ of the way up the jars. Don't put the lid on. Set your crockpot to low and leave the jars to steam overnight. The honey should melt but not boil or start to bubble. In the morning, carefully (because it will still be hot) strain the honey through a fine mesh, remove the herbs, and return to the jar. Keep it in a sealed container in the back of your kitchen cabinet so it's always on hand when you need it.

HOMEMADE ELDERFLOWER CORDIAL

This delicious and refreshing cordial should become a staple summer drink because its light flavor goes well with everything. You can mix it up with some tap water, sparkling water, lemonade, or even add it to your gin and tonic. This batch will keep for two weeks in the fridge as long as you store it in sterilized and airtight bottles.

You will need:

- 25 elderflower heads, freshly picked
- 1.5 kg of white sugar
- 1.5 l of water
- 3 lemons, sliced

Bring the water to a boil and stir in the sugar until it has all dissolved. Add it a spoonful at a time and stop when the liquid appears saturated, even if you haven't used it all yet. Put your elderflower heads and the sliced lemons into a separate bowl and pour the sugar water over the top. Leave to infuse for at least 24 hrs, then strain the liquid to remove the lemons and elderflowers. Bottle your cordial and enjoy it as a long iced drink or as a flavor shot in your favorite cocktail.

BANISH *Those Blues Smoothie*

Your throat chakra is aligned with the color blue, and blue foods can help to recharge and refresh its energy. This chakra is also helped by sea vegetables, like the spirulina used in this smoothie, because they are rich in iodine, a mineral that supports hormone production in your thyroid gland.

You will need:

- 2 cups of plant milk

- 2 frozen bananas
- 1 cup of blueberries, frozen or fresh
- ½ a cup of blackberries, frozen or fresh
- 1 ½ tsps of spirulina

Fill your blender with the ingredients and blitz on a high setting. You want this smoothie to be just that— smooth! Feel free to mix and match the berries to your own taste. Other blue fruits you could add or substitute include grapes, elderberries, and plums.

THROAT CHAKRA MEDITATION

The throat chakra is influenced by sound, so we're going to use some sound healing techniques in our meditation. If you live in a city or busy area where there is a lot of artificial ambient noise, you can do this meditation inside with a playlist of nature sounds. Some good choices are rain, waves, night insects, and forest sounds. If you live some-where quieter or near a natural space, you can make your-self comfortable outside, where you can focus on the sounds in your backyard, local park, lake, or beach. You can also daub some essential oils (diluted in a carrier oil) on your pulse points. I recommend lavender and coriander to bring calm.

- Sit on the ground with your legs crossed. Slowly circle your head in a clockwise direction, taking time to pause slightly at each of the four directional points. Repeat five times, and then do the same in a counterclockwise direction. Facing forward, inhale and shrug your shoulders up to your ears, then exhale sharply and drop them down again. Repeat five times, then return your shoulders and neck to a neutral position.

- Close your eyes and focus on the sounds around you. There's no need to listen for anything in particular, but once something catches your attention, concentrate on it and try to block out all other noises. You can use ujjayi breathing to bring the focus of your energy to your throat while you listen. Can you identify the sound? Which direction is it coming from?

- Let an image form in your mind that is related to the sound—it could be the picture of a bird, waves on the shore, or something more abstract. Imagine a blue light washing over your image. Feel the blue light bathing your mind, filling your head, and then slipping down your throat so that it sits just above your collarbone. Release this light into the world with a deep exhale, chanting the syllable *ham*. Repeat five times and slowly bring the rest of the world back into focus. Allow the other sounds around you to make themselves known, and when you are ready, open your eyes.

SMUDGING

Smudging is an effective way to use herbs to clear your meditation space of negative energy. You will need a bundle of dried sage tied with some natural twine and a small bowl of sand. Open a window, so your negative energy can leave. Light the sage and walk clockwise around the room, keeping your mind focused on positive intentions. Encourage the smoke to enter all the corners of your room, where it can chase away the negative energy. When you are finished, extinguish your bundle by stubbing it out in the sand. Smudge every week as part of your herbalist rituals to keep your home full of positive healing energy.

6

THE THIRD EYE CHAKRA

Your sixth and penultimate chakra is your third eye chakra. Located in the central point between your eyebrows, this chakra is also known as *Ajna*, which translates to "command" or "perceive." Your third eye is the seat of your brain's intuition, helping you to see into the future but also to see the truth about people and situations. Your two eyes view the physical world, but your third eye looks into the spiritual world. It is unencumbered by distractions and deceptions, as long as this chakra remains unblocked, and is an important guide as you make your way through life.

The third eye chakra is often represented by the colors indigo or purple. Both represent wisdom and spirituality, highlighting this chakra's influence over high planes and forms of consciousness.

THIRD EYE CHAKRA ASSOCIATIONS

The third eye chakra is associated with your brain; not only the well-being of the organ itself, but also all of your thoughts and dreams, as well as your intellect. You might have noticed that as we move up the chakras, the physical areas they are responsible for influencing get smaller and smaller, but their responsibility for emotional and spiritual energies increases. Along with your brain, the third eye chakra also casts its influence over the base of your skull, your ears, nose, and eyes.

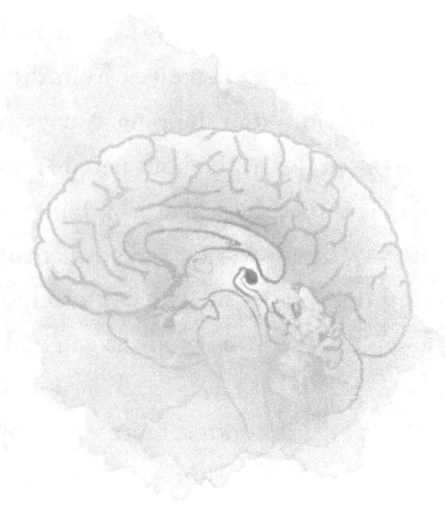

(*The Pineal Gland*)

There are two glands located in your brain that are worth singling out for their association with the third eye chakra: the pineal gland and the pituitary gland. Your pituitary gland is often referred to as the master gland because it secretes hormones that instruct many of your body's systems and functions. Your pituitary gland influences your growth, your reproductive system—it is also responsible for kicking off puberty when you reach your teenage years— and it regulates your metabolism and digestive function. The pineal gland is the regulator of your circadian rhythms; it releases melatonin at nighttime to help you sleep and serotonin during the daytime, which helps to keep your moods stable.

On the spiritual plane, your third eye chakra holds your brain's capacity for wisdom. While your throat chakra allows you to speak your truth, it is your third eye chakra that divines it in the first place. It is the source of your dreams and the ability to interpret their meaning, allowing you to accept the universe's guidance. When your chakra is balanced, you see things clearly, both in terms of recognizing the path you must take and in understanding the lessons of the past.

Your third eye chakra also looks inward, helping you to see who you really are and to understand how and why this may be different from what the world sees. When we suffer misunderstandings, it can be a sign that this chakra is not functioning correctly.

WHAT INFLUENCES THE THIRD EYE CHAKRA?

As with the throat chakra, the element that influences your third eye chakra is not one of the traditional four physical elements; however, it is one that is absolutely vital for our well-being: the element of light. Light is the source of all life on Earth. It nourishes the plants, without which there would be no oxygen, no food for the animals to eat, no plant medicines, and nothing to anchor the soil to the Earth. Light also symbolizes spiritual illumination; bringing something to light means revealing the truth, one of the core tasks of your third eye chakra.

(*Saturn*)

Other influential sources of energy for your third eye chakra are the planets Saturn and Jupiter. Jupiter rules our capacity for higher wisdom; knowing where to find it, recognizing it, and being able to apply it. It is a very energetic planet, invigorating those that are under its rule and encouraging us to look forward to a bright future. By contrast, Saturn's focus lies on the past. It also represents wisdom, but this is wisdom learned from our past and our history. The confluence of both planets powers your third eye's ability to see forward and backward through time.

(*Jupiter*)

As well as being influenced by the planets, your chakras also get their energy from the phases of the moon, with some chakras being stronger than others during different parts of the cycle. For the third eye chakra, this is the new moon. The new moon is the quietest part of the lunar cycle and a time for pause and inward reflection. Use this time to focus on clearing your third eye chakra and strengthening your connection with your intuition and perception.

The third eye chakra also has strong associations with a trio of Hindu deities: Krishna, Shiva, and Rama. There are many stories about Shiva—also known as the Destroyer and part of the Hindu holy trinity—including the legend that his third eye is so powerful he can use it to omit a deadly beam of light. Part of Shiva's purpose is to reveal the truth about people by destroying their deceptions and illusions. This aligns him most strongly with the actions of the third eye chakra.

HOW TO KNOW IF YOUR THIRD EYE CHAKRA NEEDS HELP

Like all the other chakras, an imbalance in your third eye chakra can affect the way you behave and the way that you feel. When your chakra is well-balanced and energized, you will have an open mind, capable of looking at things from multiple angles and accepting and understanding the views of others. You will also be inwardly aware and able to reflect on your own thoughts, feelings, and actions. A balanced third eye chakra brings good dreams and a certain amount of psychic intuition because you are able to see and hear messages in the spiritual realm.

However, if your third eye chakra is blocked or over-stimulated, you might experience some of these signs:

- Becoming obsessed with something, or finding your focus becoming extremely narrow, are signs of an unhealthy third eye chakra. It's one thing to have hobbies and interests, but if they start consuming all of your energy and taking up so much time that the rest of your life starts to suffer, then your third eye probably needs rebalancing. This narrow focus can also turn inwards, leading you to become self-serving and self-righteous.

- Having nightmares, which can be an indication that communication between your third eye chakra and the spiritual world is malfunctioning. Your chakra misinterprets messages, leaving you with frightening imagery and dark omens. Delusions and hallucinations while waking may also indicate third-eye chakra problems.

- An inability to put yourself in someone else's shoes and see other interpretations. In conversations, you will steadfastly stick to your opinion: this indicates a closed mind that refuses to acknowledge wider possibilities.

- Repeating the same mistakes over and over again. Having a deficient third eye chakra makes it difficult to connect your actions with their outcomes, which in turn makes learning from your past impossible. If you look back through your life and spot a pattern—maybe dating the same toxic people or stumbling at the same hurdle at work—your third eye chakra probably needs a tune-up.

- When your third eye chakra isn't functioning properly, it interrupts the flow of life energy around your energy body. This can cause physical symptoms as well as behavioral changes. Signs that your third eye chakra is blocked include:

- Recurring headaches and migraines. These headaches indicate a build-up of negative and stagnant energy around your third eye chakra. Imagine it like a traffic jam of thoughts and messages with nowhere to go—no wonder it hurts.

- Eye problems, from long-term issues like myopia to recurring swellings and irritation. I'm not promising that a balanced chakra will stop you from needing glasses, but it will maintain your eye health and stop existing issues from progressing.

- Sleep disorders like insomnia, narcolepsy, difficulty staying asleep, and tossing and turning in bed. These are down to a disruption to your pineal gland and its function as a sleep regulator.

THE PINEAL GLAND: NATURE'S ALARM CLOCK

Your body has a number of glands, and each is responsible for releasing a different hormone. The pineal gland isn't very well known, but it is one of the most important. Nestled in your brain, it is light-sensitive and secretes different hormones depending on the time of day: mela-tonin at night, which helps your body to go to sleep, and serotonin during the day, which regulates your mood, emotions, and bodily processes.

Melatonin is important because it is the single biggest contributor to our sleep cycles. It is produced in response to darkness, and therefore the levels of melatonin in your body are highest in the nighttime. High melatonin levels make you feel sleepy, which prepares your body for a night of rest. Throughout the night, your levels drop, and by the time you wake up, there should be very little or no melatonin left. If you find you are sluggish in the morning and take a while to feel energized, it means there is still too much melatonin in your bloodstream. If you sleep badly, wake frequently, or find it difficult to get to sleep in the first place, then it is likely that you haven't got enough melatonin at night. Melatonin production can be affected by artificial light because your pineal gland doesn't recognize that it is nighttime.

Your pineal gland can suffer from calcification, which is a build-up of calcium phosphate crystals. This calcification can inhibit its functions and lead to sleep problems. It is also a symptom of a blocked third eye chakra, and you can decalcify it by stimulating and restoring balance to the chakra:

- Take gotu kola supplement. This herb repairs damaged nerves, increases oxygen supply to the brain, and fortifies the pineal gland.
- Eat an organic, plant-based diet. Processed foods and foods with lots of extra additives can increase calcification, so get as much chemical-free, fresh food as possible.

- While lying in the dark, place a crystal in the center of your third eye. Choose one that is indigo or purple to properly stimulate your chakra. Good crystals for this purpose include amethyst, lapis lazuli, sodalite, and moonstone. Leave it there for up to 30 minutes while listening to a relaxing meditation.
- Diffuse some essential oils that have an affinity with your third eye chakra. These include sandalwood, pine, clary sage, and myrrh.

THIRD EYE HEALING WITH NATURE

These herbs have been around for thousands of years, and we can't begin to comprehend how much wisdom and energy they have absorbed from the universe during that time. Plants can offer us so much more than just physical nourishment, and those plants that are attuned to your third eye chakra are particularly nourishing for the mind and spirit. Whenever you have a problem with your dreams, your sleep, or your connection with the wider universe, you'll be in good hands if you turn to one of these herbs for help. Some can be found at your local drugstore, while others will have to be ordered from one of a number of specialist online sites. You might even want to try growing them yourself: you will not only benefit from the harvested herb's medicinal powers, but you will also be able to build a stronger bond with them by sitting and talking to them as they grow. This will enhance your herb's healing powers even more.

Mugwort (Artemisia Vulgaris)

Mugwort is native to Europe and Asia, where it has been used for thousands of years in traditional herbalist practices. When settlers immigrated to North America, they took mugwort plants with them, and it has now made itself at home on those shores too. Unfortunately, mugwort has made a name for itself as a prolific weed, meaning it is rarely welcome in people's gardens and actively treated with herbicides when spotted. If you do choose to grow mugwort at home, it is best contained in a pot, where its root systems cannot become too invasive and damage the other nearby plants. It will happily grow anywhere and under any conditions.

Although it blooms from mid-summer through fall, mugwort's flowers are a rarity because they lack petals, appearing instead as simple yellowish-green buds. The long, thin flowers of this plant are most striking as their under-sides have a silvery appearance due to being covered in hairs. These leaves rise all the way up mugwort's tall stems, alternating sides as they climb. The whole herb is used for herbalist medicines: the roots, stems, leaves, and flowers are dried or powdered, and essential oils are extracted from the leaves.

Mugwort is ruled by the moon, the celestial body that also reigns over the pineal gland. This emphasizes the strong bond between mugwort and your third eye chakra. Mugwort has a number of affinities, including the liver, digestive system, and female reproductive system, but it is also a hugely beneficial sleep aid. Often called the 'dream herb,' mugwort not only helps you find it easier to fall asleep, but it also stimulates and energizes your subconscious mind, triggering wave after wave of incredibly vivid dreams. Some people even find that mugwort encourages lucid dreaming. However, all this nighttime entertainment can have its downside because you could wake up feeling mentally exhausted.

Dreams are important because they allow us to connect with and explore the spiritual realm. They are how the universe sends us messages and where your brain processes and learns from the events of the day. Mugwort is particularly effective for people who find themselves wandering through life in a dreamlike state, as it can ground them to reality. It also works well to calm the anxieties of people who struggle with sensory processing and find that the world can be too loud and energetic.

Because mugwort exists as a wild weed, it should be easy to find and wildcraft. Check around for any wild and neglected green spaces local to you, even if they are just grassy verges, and you might get lucky. Remember not to take everything away with you, but leave some for other wildcrafters. You can hang the stems up to dry or use the fresh leaves in tinctures. Many recipes from traditional Chinese medicine involve burning the dried leaves and using them to bring warmth back to stiff joints.

Mugwort is generally safe for most people to take, although if you know you are allergic to ragweed, you will find it also brings on a reaction. Because this herb can affect the uterus, it shouldn't be taken while pregnant, and it is probably best avoided during breastfeeding as well.

SHANKHPUSHPI (CONVOLVULUS PLURICAULIS)

This herb has many names, including shankhahuli, sankali, and English speedwheel. They all describe the unique appearance of the flowers, which is similar to an iris, except rounder. A large, ovoid outer petal surrounds a pair of smaller inner petals, draped asymmetrically like a long cape. These petals can be either white or indigo blue, with a yellow inner streak. Shankhpushpi is a low plant, spreading across the ground rather than rising up tall, with tiny green leaves that are often less than one inch long. It is native to India, but other varieties of *convolvulus* are found all over the world.

Shankhpushpi plants grow well in tubs and can be a colorful and cheerful addition to any garden, yard, or city balcony. They need to be kept warm, though, preferring 70-85 °F, and their soil mustn't be allowed to dry out. Plant seeds indoors in propagator trays to ensure the growth of healthy seedlings, then plant out once they have reached a few inches in height. Harvest flowers, leaves, stalks, and roots from January to May.

This herb has been used in Ayurvedic practices for thousands of years. It will work as a maintaining tonic for your consciousness and will keep your mind in great condition. It is also known for its ability to improve your memory and support the growth of intelligence. Shankhpushpi can help you to concentrate better and restore energy to a brain that is feeling fatigued. It also helps to ward off depression, anxiety, insomnia, and forms of stress.

Shankhpushpi is recommended for us when working with the third eye chakra because its restorative properties improve a number of important brain functions. This helps to clear any energy blockages that can build up because of faulty neural pathways. When your spiritual energy field is thoroughly cleansed, you open yourself up to receiving clearer messages from the universe and will find yourself more creatively and spiritually inspired.

Some of the main chemicals that shankhpushpi is harvested for include alkaloids called convolvuline and shankhapushpine. This herb also contains volatile oils, flavonoids, sucrose, starch, and proteins. In Ayurvedic terms, it is a cooling, sweet herb that is evident in its calming abilities. Shankhpushpi not only calms your nervous system, reducing stress, anxiety, and restlessness, but it also promotes natural sleep, making it an effective herbal treatment for insomnia.

Shankhpushpi is considered safe to take during pregnancy; in fact, it can have a strengthening effect on the uterine muscles. But as always, you should check with your healthcare professional before taking supplements. Shankhpushpi may cause hypotension in people with low blood pressure, so it is not recommended for people with this condition, even if they are on medication to treat it.

LAVENDER (LAVANDULA ANGUSTIFOLIA)

Lavender is the second herb in our list to share its color with the third eye chakra. This wonderfully fragrant shrub is found growing wild in the mountainous Mediterranean regions of Europe, but it is also farmed in the rest of Europe and as far afield as Australia. There are other variants that are native to North Africa and Western Asia, but this is the most commonly recognized of all the lavenders.

Lavender is an evergreen shrub that flowers throughout the summer months. It is hugely attractive to bees and other pollinators, grows quickly and easily in well-drained soil, and produces the most beautiful flowers atop its long, thin stalks. Lavender leaves are short and thin, resembling slender needles, and their color is that of a dusky silvery green.

The most common use of lavender is for its scent, as an essential oil, or using dried flowers. You will often find lavender added to commercial products such as wheat pillows, bath oils, and baby powder. It has a cleansing aroma that relays its antiseptic and antibacterial properties. It is also extremely relaxing and soothing due to its sedative qualities—these are so strong that you don't even need to take the herb; just its scent will weave a magical, calming spell.

Dried flowers and stalks yield the most essential oil—about 3%—but they also contain other chemicals, such as linalyl acetate, which gives the flowers their distinctive smell; cineol, which contributes to the antimicrobial properties of lavender; and tannins, which are antibacterial. While these chemicals all help lavender to cleanse and clear away germs and microbes in the body, lavender is also good for clearing your mind and removing stress, anxiety, and feelings of depression. Lavender also works to clear mental blockages that result in headaches.

A cooling and drying herb, lavender is also an excellent tonic for sleep. By acting to remove the stressors of the day, it prepares the body and brain to enter the sleep state in a way that they are receptive to dreams and messages directed towards your subconscious. Lavender has been used for many years as a gateway herb, bringing greater spiritual understanding and leaving the way clear for intuitive visions to make themselves known. It is an herb ruled by Mercury, the planet of the mind and communication, and nowhere is this more obvious than when considering lavender's ability to bring mental clarity and spiritual awareness.

Lavender is such a gentle herb that there are no contraindications, meaning it can be used by children, during pregnancy, and by people who suffer from other medical complaints. Those who have a dry constitution may find they want to combine lavender with moist herbs to balance its drying effect or take it as a tea so you are hydrating your body at the same time.

EYEBRIGHT (EUPHRASIA OFFICINALIS)

This small, dainty flowering herb comes from Europe, where it can be found growing in unexpected spots: neglected meadows with poor-quality soil, sandy, rocky outcrops, and anywhere else where the soil is well-drained. Eyebright doesn't need nutrient-rich soil because it is parasitic and feeds off the neighboring plants and grass. For this important reason, you might want to avoid growing eyebright on its own in a pot, but it will thrive in a mixed herbaceous border.

Eyebright can grow as tall as 12 in. and will flower from July to September. Its flowers are the origin of this plant's descriptive moniker because they are supposed to resemble a human eye. The flowers themselves have two white petals, one larger than the other, forming an asymmetrical bell shape. The inside of the flowers has vibrant purple veins and a central yellow spot. The leaves, shoots, flowers, and stems are all harvested for medicinal use. They contain tannins, flavonoids, saponins, essential oils, important minerals including iron and zinc, and vitamins A, C, D, and E.

In the 16th century, eyebright was declared an eye herb because of its flowers: This sounds like a weak connection, but the herbalists of the time got it absolutely right. It has an anti-inflammatory quality, combined with astringent and antiseptic properties, which make it the go-to herb for treating eye conditions. Eyebright can clear up styes, reinvigorate tired and aching eyes, and has proved successful in treating cases of conjunctivitis and blepharitis.

The connection of eyebright to the third chakra goes back to ancient folklore when people believed that carrying pouches of eyebright would grant you the gift of second sight. These flowers could clear your third eye chakra of any blockages or cloudiness and enable you to see through the lies of people around you. If you wanted to know which neighbor stole your chicken, this was what the village herbalists would recommend.

Eyebright is a bit of a contradiction, as it has cooling energies, but it is also ruled by the sun, which traditionally aligns with heating and dry herbs. The cooling, astringent properties of eyebright help it to reduce inflammation and close the skin cells to protect against further issues. The sun influences eyebright's work in the spiritual realm because it inspires you to find your true self and gives you the courage to reveal it to the world.

As with most herbs, you should consult with your doctor before taking eyebright if you are pregnant or breast-feeding. This is due to a lack of research and medical studies on the potential effects. If you are using eyebright as an eyebath or on a compress, remember to use a fresh solution each time to avoid contamination.

RECIPES AND RELAXATION

(Third) Eye Opening Morning Smoothie

While a lot of third-eye chakra herbs focus on helping you sleep, that's only half of the cycle. Better melatonin regulation will help you wake up feeling revitalized, but a good dose of purple foods for breakfast will make sure that your chakra is wide awake too. You can play around with the ingredients of this smoothie as it suits you. Some alternative fruits to use include plums, damsons, blackberries, elderberries, black grapes, and elderberries.

You will need:

- 1 cup of figs, fresh is best
- 1 cup of frozen banana slices

- ½ cup of frozen blueberries
- 1 cup of natural yogurt, vanilla flavor
- 1 tbsp honey

Remove any stalks and seeds from your fruits and tip them into a blender, followed by the yogurt and honey. Blitz until smooth, probably for around 2-3 minutes. If you prefer a thicker or thinner smoothie, adjust the volume of yogurt.

Lavender and Chamomile Bedtime Brew

This unbeatable combination of soothing, relaxing herbs will have even the most stressed-out insomniac sleeping like a baby in no time. Brew yourself a cup at the end of a particularly stressful day to help slip into a world of pleasant, vivid dreams, and let your subconscious process its thoughts in peace.

You will need:

- 1 tsp of dried lavender flowers
- 1 tsp of dried chamomile flowers.
- 8 oz of water

Spoon your dried flowers into a tea strainer or empty tea bag and pop them into your favorite mug. You could also make a steeping bundle by tying them in a circle of cheesecloth. Heat the water on the stove until it boils, then pour it into your mug. Drop in the herbs and leave to steep for 10 minutes. Remove the strainer, bag, or bundle and discard. Sink into your comfiest chair, close your eyes, and sip slowly.

Sweet Dreams Pillow Pouch

Some herbs are so powerful that they will work simply by being within our energy field or through the inhalation of their scent. If you want to ensure a good night's sleep full of vivid dreams, then try crafting this herbal pouch. Alternatively, you could just hang the mugwort over your bed, but the addition of the other herbs will help you relax and drift off to an easy sleep.

You will need:

- A few sprigs of dried mugwort
- A cup of dried lavender flowers

- A cup of dried chamomile flowers

Break the mugwort into small pieces and mix together with the other herbs. Pour into a bag made of breathable material like 100% cotton, linen, or cheesecloth, and tie it shut. You could add a drop of lavender essential oil to accentuate the natural scent of the dried herbs, but this is not necessary, as they will be fragrant on their own. Place the pouch on your bedside table, hang it above your bed, or even tuck them inside your pillowcase. Shake occasionally to reawaken the herb and prevent its energies from stagnating.

THIRD EYE CHAKRA MEDITATION

For this meditation, we're going to practice a technique called Alternate Nostril Breathing or *Nadi Shodhana*. It is a wonderful way to quieten an overactive mind by restoring balance to your thoughts. The nose is connected to your third eye chakra, so you know the effects are going straight to the source.

How to perform *Nadi Shodhana*:

1. Close both nostrils with your index finger and thumb.
2. Open your left nostril and breath in.
3. Close your left nostril with your finger (or thumb, depending on which hand you're using), open your right nostril, and breathe out.

4. Pause for a second
5. Inhale through the right nostril
6. Close the right nostril, open the left nostril, and breathe out.

This counts as one cycle of Nadi Shodhana (Alternate Nostril Breathing)

To FURTHER ENHANCE the effectiveness of this meditation on your third eye chakra, and specifically your pineal gland, you might want to sit in a darkened room. You can diffuse some essential oils—frankincense is good, as is lavender—to help you relax. Alternatively, make up a potpourri bowl of purple flowers like lavender, violets, borage, and passion-flower. Leave the bowl where the scent can fill the room.

Sit in a comfortable and supported position. Take your dominant hand and place your second and third fingers between your eyebrows, where they can rest just above your third eye chakra. You can also press your tongue against the roof of your mouth to connect with your chakra from below. You'll want to use your thumb and fourth finger to close alternate nostrils as you breathe in a cycle.

Begin by taking a deep breath as normal. Pause slightly before exhaling, then use your thumb or fourth finger—it will depend on which hand you used—to close off your right nostril. Now inhale through your left nostril, pausing slightly at the top of the inhale. Switch fingers and breathe out through your right nostril. Try to keep the length and depth of your breaths as even as possible. If it helps, you could set some rhythmic gong sounds to trigger your breaths.

Repeat on the other side: breathe in through your right nostril, pause at the top, and breathe out through the left. This completes one cycle of breaths. Repeat for a total of 10 cycles. You should feel relaxed, and your brain should feel uncluttered. This is a good preparation for sleep and is best performed as part of your nighttime ritual. Take a few final deep breaths, chanting *om* on each exhalation.

THE CROWN CHAKRA

Your final chakra is your crown chakra, also known as Sahasrara, and it is located at the top of your skull. This chakra represents higher knowledge and enlightenment, as well as being the embodiment of your spiritual identity. Physically it is aligned with your hair, skin, nails, nervous system, and brain.

The crown chakra and third eye chakra are the two chakras that are most connected with the spiritual plane. Where the third eye chakra allows you to see messages and signs from the universe and the divine, your crown chakra gives you the wisdom to understand them and to grow from them. It is through the crown chakra that you will find your place in the world, as you understand that we are all parts of a cosmic jigsaw, each important in its own right, even if you can't see why yet.

Different schools of thought describe the crown chakra as associated with either the color white (if your third eye chakra was purple) or the color violet (if your third eye chakra was indigo). Violet is a deeply spiritual color with a unifying nature that brings together elements of the other chakras. White symbolizes the divine light and connection to a higher plane of existence. It is also a unification of all the other colors yet remains the symbol of purity.

CROWN CHAKRA ASSOCIATIONS

The third eye chakra is responsible for most of the sensory organs (eyes, ears, tongue, and nose), but your crown chakra influences the largest of them all: the skin. The largest organ in your body, the skin, is covered in touch receptors that constantly remind you that you are here and you are interacting with the world. Imagine how weird it would feel to walk barefoot on the ground but not feel the grass, the warmth, or even the pressure against your sole. Your skin is your first contact with reality; it's your main grounding organ.

Linked to your skin is your nervous system. In fact, your nervous system is linked to everything, sending and receiving millions of quick electrical signals from your brain every day. I've already mentioned how your heart's intelligence triggers the brain to send out signals, but it isn't the only organ to do so. Your nervous system will carry messages to the brain that you are hungry, in pain, or scared, and it will also bring back the messages to swallow food, retract your foot from the pin you stepped on, or run from a tiger.

Your brain is another organ connected to your crown chakra. We've already seen how the third eye chakra influences the communication and interpretation centers of your brain, but it has far more functions than just that. Your crown chakra exerts its power over the memory centers of your brain, as well as reigning over your concentration and focus, and innate intelligence.

Your crown chakra is also the connection between your physical self, your energy body, and your spiritual self. It is here where all these different aspects come together to form the whole self, and at this point of convergence, you are open to receiving the cosmic energy of the universe. Think of your crown chakra as a gateway for divine energy, where all the wisdom of the spirits and the universe can flow into you, and you can send your energy out into the ether.

WHAT INFLUENCES THE CROWN CHAKRA?

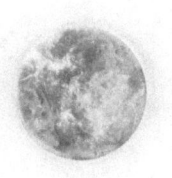

Unlike the other chakras, your crown chakra has no influential element. Instead, it is powered and guided by the spirit of the universe and the energies of those around you. A hugely influential power over this chakra is the Sun. As the star at the center of our solar system, the Sun contains a phenomenal amount of energy that travels for distances greater than we can comprehend. The Sun touches all aspects of not only our world but those around us, just like divine and cosmic energy brings light into our bodies. It symbolizes the life force that powers our physical selves and the energy that nourishes our spiritual side.

The Hindu deity most often associated with the crown chakra is Nataraja, known as the Cosmic Dancer. Nataraja is another form of Shiva the Destroyer, but he embodies all that is joyful and good about the creation that rises from the ashes. He is often depicted in various dancing poses, adorned with elements of the cosmos, like the moon on his crown and the sacred Ganges river in his hair. Nataraja brings together different parts of creation, just as the crown chakra unifies the parts that make you whole.

The New Moon

The crown chakra is also strongly aligned with the lunar phase of the new moon. As the skies are their darkest around this time, we are more able to see some of the faintest stars that are otherwise hidden from view. Your crown chakra helps you to see and interpret hidden messages, especially those that come out of dark times to bring us valuable lessons. It is an acknowledgment that darkness and death are invaluable parts of light and birth and a time to pause and consider your place in the grand scheme of the cosmos.

HOW TO KNOW IF YOUR CROWN CHAKRA NEEDS HELP

If your crown chakra is balanced, you will experience an overwhelming feeling of peace and a closeness with your spiritual side. You won't have anxieties about your purpose, instead feeling completely settled, like a solid table that is grounded and balanced on all sides and capable of bearing the weight of everything it has to carry. Not only this, but you will feel able to impart the wisdom of your enlightenment to others, guiding and teaching them in a way that is diplomatic and wise, rather than patronizing, lecturing, and condescending.

However, when your crown chakra is out of alignment or blocked, this can produce a number of undesirable behavioral and physical symptoms. A blockage here can mean your connection to your spiritual self, or the universe, has been severed, and can leave you feeling untethered and unstable. Other things to look out for include:

- A general disdain for spiritual people and their practices, or alienation from beliefs you previously held. This should be a massive red flag that your relationship with your spiritual self and the cosmic energy of the universe is faltering.

- Alternatively, blindly following the advice and teaching of anyone who purports to be a spiritual leader or wise person. This can also lead to extreme behavior in an attempt to reconnect with your spiritual self, including vows of silence, meditation marathons, and unhealthy amounts of fasting.

- Trying to reopen a connection to the spiritual and divine energies through rituals. This can lead to an almost obsessive-compulsive routine of yoga, meditation, essential oils, praying, spells, and mantras, which is so all-encompassing that it interferes with living your life.

- Feeling distant and confused, as if you can feel that something is missing from your life but cannot identify what. It's that feeling when you walk into a room and forget why; only it continues throughout your entire day.

- It's easy to focus on how your crown chakra powers your spiritual self and forget that it is also responsible for guiding some fairly large systems in your body as well. When the energy to these parts of your body is blocked, it can manifest as mental and physical problems like:

- Chronic exhaustion. If you feel tired all the time, no matter how much sleep, exercise, and fresh air you get, it could be a sign of spiritual exhaustion. Try using a combination of third eye and crown chakra herbs to inspire a more restful slumber and recharge your spiritual connection.

- Skin conditions such as acne, eczema, and dermatitis can signify a blocked crown chakra. I've already mentioned several herbs throughout these chapters that can have a cooling and soothing effect on the skin, such as mullein, peppermint, rose, hibiscus, red clover, and marshmallow. These can be used to calm down any irritation while you work on reenergizing your crown chakra and repairing the root of the problem.

- Memory loss and other problems can also reveal a stuttering crown chakra. You might find you repeat yourself in conversations or forget the point you were trying to make. Losing items like your keys, glasses, and shoes become more frequent occurrences, and you will need to write down important dates or risk missing a birthday or anniversary.

- As well as feeling disconnected from your spiritual side, you may experience feelings of disconnection physically. Pins and needles in your limbs or loss of sensation are common in people with blocked crown chakras.

USING HERBS TO UNBLOCK YOUR CROWN CHAKRA

Because your crown chakra influences a number of physical and spiritual elements of your being, it is unlikely that you will find one herb that works as a remedy for all of them. Although many herbs, especially adaptogens, have a number of effects on the body, they will usually have a main target that herbalists feel they work most closely with. For general crown chakra support, remember to eat foods that have a deep purple or white color because this chakra is associated with both. Cook with eggplants, purple cabbage, cauliflower, or onions, and snack on fruits like blackberries, purple grapes, and plums. You could even make your own herb-infused honey using lavender or violets—you can adapt the Superhoney recipe from the throat chakra recipes.

Herbs for the Nervous System

Your nervous system is how your body communicates how it is feeling. Without your nerves, you wouldn't feel pleasure or pain or enjoy the many physical sensations your brain processes throughout the day. We use our sense of touch to feel calm and safe; under weighted blankets, stroking pets, or holding the hand of a loved one. So much of our identity and our feelings are abstract, existing inside our heads, hearts, and chakras, that we need the sense of touch to remember that we are rooted in a physical world. When this starts to falter, it can lead to feelings of disassociation.

Herbs that have nervine qualities specifically support your nervous system. Some will keep it maintained and in good health, while others will relax and calm nerves that have become over-sensitive or restore balance to the system as a whole. For a general nervine tonic, try mimosa (not the cocktail) or bacopa. For nervines to relax and restore, look at lemon balm and California poppy.

Herbs for the Skin

An extension of your nervous system, keeping your skin in good condition helps you to fully experience the world around you. But your skin is also your body's protector, keeping your insides inside. When the skin is broken, bacteria and other pathogens may find a way inside, bringing infection and irritation. Again, these herbs can be broken down into those herbs that can be used every day to maintain skin health and those that are used to treat specific instances of irritation or upset. You can even find herbs that promote the rapid healing of wounds, ensuring that your natural armor is back to top condition quickly.

Herbs that make excellent skin tonics include oat straw and horsetail. Healing herbs to treat skin conditions include aloe vera and dandelion. If you want herbs to treat injuries and skin breakages, turn to calendula and turmeric.

Herbs for Mental Clarity

We couldn't discuss the crown chakra without mentioning your brain. It is your central processor and is responsible for keeping track of your thoughts and planning your actions. Your crown chakra influences the parts of your brain that deal with memory, focus, and intellect. Taking herbs to maintain these aspects on a daily basis is thought to be able to delay the effects of aging, keeping your brain working better for longer. In fact, the herb gotu kola has even been linked with a reduction in Alzheimer's symptoms (Wattanathorn et al., 2008).

It goes without saying that mental health is incredibly important to our general well-being, so making sure your crown chakra is fully open is a top priority. Rosemary and ginseng are both excellent brain tonics to maintain function and improve your focus. If you need a mental health lift, eleuthero root and bacopa both have antidepressant properties and will clear mental fog and recharge your energy levels.

CROWN CHAKRA HEALING WITH NATURE

Eastern medicine has a longer history of spiritualism than Western medicine, so herbs that support your spiritual health often have their origins in India, China, and other parts of Asia. The majority of these herbs come from Ayurvedic medicine and traditional Chinese medicine, making them difficult to wildcraft and forage in other parts of the world. Many can be cultivated in your garden if you want a small supply nearby, but by far, the easiest way to get hold of any is from a good internet supplier, your local apothecary, or a neighborhood drugstore.

I mentioned in the introduction that spiritual herbalists will often encourage you to look for herbs that have an affinity with your own ancestry. If this is not possible, you could form a stronger bond with your herbs by growing your own and taking time to commune with them before harvesting.

Gotu Kola (Centella Asiatica)

Gotu kola is a member of the parsley family of plants and is native to a number of counties in the Southern Hemisphere, including India, China, Australia, Madagascar, and South Africa. It is one of the go-to herbs for many Ayurvedic practitioners when they need a rejuvenating tonic for the brain.

This small plant has distinctive green leaves shaped like

round lily pads. Each leaf tops an individual thin stalk. These leaves are the parts of the plant that are used herbally, and they can be beneficial, either fresh or dried. Growing gotu kola in your own garden, either in a bed or in a pot, is really easy. They love a warmer climate—or you could grow them inside—but you must make sure that the soil is never allowed to dry out. Once the plants are happily established, they can grow aggressively, so it might be beneficial to make sure they are well-contained, or your neighbors might not be so happy.

Ancient herbalists used to believe that the look or color of a herb would tell you what it was best suited to treat. They said that the gotu kola leaf resembles the brain and its two hemispheres, and they would use it to restore balance between them. Gotu kola was also traditionally used by monks and Yogis to help them to focus better while meditating, and many still use it in their rituals today. It has also been used as a tonic for blood flow, as it can make your vein walls stronger.

The active constituents of gotu kola include flavonols, amino acids, sterols, and a number of saponins, including asiaticoside, madecassoside, and madasiatic acid. Because of these, Gotu kola is an amazing antioxidant and detoxifier that has so many benefits for your brain: it reduces brain fog, increases your ability to concentrate, improves your memory, and even prevents brain cells from being attacked by free radicals.

Gotu kola is also used effectively as an antidepressant and antianxiety herb. It produces a mild sedative, which is calming and soothing to your nerves: this reduces feelings of anxiety and the hyper-awareness that these emotions can bring. Gotu kola also calms and sharpens the mind by encouraging neural nerves to grow and spread.

According to Ayurveda, gotu kola has a cooling energy, which supports its work as an antioxidant. It also corresponds to the planet Mercury, the ruler of the mind and the nervous system. Mercury herbs bring clarity to anyone who uses them, as they open the brain to the senses and make it more aware of the world around you through the sensations they process.

Because gotu kola works as a sedative, it should not be taken in conjunction with other tranquilizers or sedatives. It should also be avoided during pregnancy or while breast-feeding because not enough research has been done on the effects it can have during these times. You should also not take gotu kola if you are on medication for diabetes, high cholesterol, or liver problems—talk to your doctor about the interactions, and they might be able to adjust your doses accordingly.

BACOPA (BACOPA MONNIERI)

Bacopa and gotu kola are used interchangeably in ancient Ayurvedic texts because their interactions with the body are very similar. In fact, both were given the name *Brahmi*, which refers to their alignment with the Hindu deity Brahma, who, in the form of Brahman, is often called the "cosmic consciousness." No wonder, then, that these herbs are related to knowledge and spiritual intelligence, both promoting a state of higher consciousness and a deeper relationship with the universe.

This herb comes from Sri Lanka and India, but it can also now be found growing in Australia and the coastal regions of the southern U.S. Bacopa loves wetlands and can be found growing in ponds and swamps. It has small, light green leaves and delicate white flowers that are made up of 5 petals. The whole plant can be dried and used medicinally, or the aerial parts—those that grow above the ground —can be enjoyed fresh.

Bacopa is another staple of Ayurvedic medicine, where it has been used for thousands of years as a rasayana, which means rejuvenating tonic. People would use this herb to encourage a long life and a bright intellect, but they would also use it specifically to improve their memory and concentration span. It is also another herb like gotu kola that can be used to protect your brain against the withering effects of aging and certain neurological impairments. Bacopa also works on your crown chakra by calming your thoughts if they become intrusive, harmful, or overbearing. By releasing these pent-up emotions in the brain, it brings clarity and allows your connection with the spiritual plane to be restored.

Another cooling herb, bacopa, also has antioxidant properties, but it is more well-known as a nervine and adaptogen. Being an adaptogen means it can alter the way it helps your body to match what is needed. This is why it is viewed as a super herb that can target multiple parts of the body, including the gastrointestinal system, the brain, the nervous system, and the liver. This herb is full of different saponins that work to increase activity in the memory areas of the brain, as well as make nerves more effective at sending their signals. One saponin called bacosine even acts as a painkiller, which supports the nervous system by calming down angry pain receptors.

Bacopa is generally considered safe for everyone, even children. In fact, it is often used by herbalists for children who have ADHD to help them find their calm. Not a lot is known about bacopa's effects during pregnancy or breastfeeding, so it is best avoided here until more research is done.

Tulsi (Ocimum Tenuiflorum)

Another herb native to India, tulsi, is sometimes called holy basil or sacred basil, and there's a good reason for this. In traditional Hindu beliefs, the tulsi plant represents the goddess Tulsi herself and is actually infused with her spirit. Planting tulsi bushes outside your house is believed to stop negative energy from reaching your door, and this herb protects your spiritual energy in the same way. Tulsi is an uplifting herb and a mood booster that actually reduces the levels of the stress hormone cortisol in your brain: This will make you feel less anxious, more balanced, and able to face the world with a smile on your face.

Like other members of the mint family, tulsi is wonderfully aromatic and makes a lovely addition to any garden, balcony, or windowsill. Just walking past is enough for you to take in the scent excreted by the essential oils in the leaves. There are a number of different varieties of tulsi, including one that has purple edges to its leaves that match the stalks of purple flowers borne by each plant. Some can bear the cold better than others, so unless you live in a region that is permanently warm, you will have to either grow tulsi indoors or choose a hardy variety. Plant in early summer in a position that enjoys full sun all day long. Tulsi is only an annual, meaning you will have to replant your crop every year, but the numerous benefits of this wonderful crown chakra herb make it worthwhile.

According to Ayurveda, tulsi is a warming herb and a restorative tonic. Another adaptogen, it has beneficial effects on many hormones in the body, helping to bring them back into balance and combating weight gain, fatigue, depression, and insomnia in the process. Unsurprisingly, tulsi is also aligned with the planet Mercury, as it looks to balance and free the mind from energy blockages. Tulsi unblocks your spiritual mind, leaving you open to new experiences, opinions, and realizations. It is often taken as a refreshing tea, either on its own or combined with cooling herbs like gotu kola or lavender.

Tulsi contains a number of beneficial chemicals, but what makes this herb unique is that each plant contains these chemicals in different amounts, even if two seemingly identical herbs are growing right next to each other. Chemicals like cineole and camphene help unblock your nose and break up mucus in your lungs, while linalool combats depression and insomnia.

As with many other herbs, the effects of tulsi during pregnancy and breastfeeding are undocumented, so it is best avoided or only used if recommended by your doctor. Tulsi is known to affect blood clotting and should not be taken by anyone with an existing clotting disorder or if you are preparing to have surgery.

CALENDULA (CALENDULA OFFICINALIS)

This vibrant and cheerful herb brings joy wherever it grows. Large yellow and orange flowers, green stalks, and feathery leaves make it distinctive and easily recognizable. Also called common marigold, this plant is native to Southern Europe, but it has been transplanted pretty much everywhere and grows well in most temperate regions. Everyone would benefit from having some in their garden, whether they plan on using them medicinally or not. Sow marigold seeds in April for flowers from June until the arrival of winter frosts. Flowers will ripen into seeds in early fall, and, if allowed, the plants will sow the next crop, ready to keep you smiling the following year.

The flowers and leaves are used for their medicinal purposes. Try to avoid supplements that just have the petals, as the most valuable parts of the flowers are the green involucres that join the petals to the stalks. These cheerful blooms used to be made into a tonic for the spirits, as well as finding their way into many different herbal medicines. A calendula infusion works wonders at reducing fever and speeding up the recovery from childhood diseases like measles and chickenpox.

Where calendula really shows its usefulness is as a topical treatment for a number of skin ailments. In centuries past, people would rub the whole flower onto bee and wasp stings in order to stop them from swelling. Nowadays, you will find calendula oil in lotions and eye washes because of its anti-inflammatory qualities. Calendula also works on cuts and wounds to aid in quick healing and to stop them from bleeding. Plus, its antiseptic qualities keep wounds clean and clear of infection—calendula is the one-stop shop for all your first aid needs.

Calendula is a cooling herb used to combat the high temperatures caused by fevers and inflammations, yet it is influenced by the sun. The sun works in an atypical way with calendula: rather than aligning with warming energetics, it imbues this herb with joyful energy and inspires its helpful, healing nature. Calendula is made up of more than thirty different chemical constituents, including essential oils, sterols, flavonoids, and glycosides.

Depending on where you live, you may or may not be able to find calendula growing in the wild. It thrives in meadows and sparse woodlands in Europe and the southern U.S., but further north, it will be less common. If you do find a crop nearby, remember to only take a small amount of the flower heads so that they can see the next generation of plants and repopulate their colony.

Calendula is considered safe for all adults and children to take unless you have an allergy to plants of the Aster-aceae family (such as chamomile and echinacea), of which it is a part. It is not recommended to take calendula during pregnancy because it has a stimulating effect on the uterus that can cause bleeding. You are, however, absolutely fine to use it topically in creams and ointments.

RECIPES AND RELAXATION

Tempting Tulsi Tea

This herb does a little bit of everything, including bringing you joy. Relaxing with a cup of this uplifting brew will help you to unwind at the end of a stressful day, reducing cortisol levels in your brain and setting you up for a good night's rest. This is the basic recipe, but you can experiment and add partner herbs according to your taste. Tulsi can have a bitter taste, so adding herbs with sweet energetics like hibiscus, rose, peppermint, and milk thistle, will not only balance this out but also give you an added boost of herbal goodness. This recipe makes two cups, so you can either share with a friend or reheat one later.

You will need:

- 2 ½ cups of water,
- 8 tulsi leaves
- 1 in. of dried ginger root, shopped
- 2 tsp of honey
- 1 tsp of lemon juice

Pop the water on the stove and add the tulsi and ginger root. Bring to a boil and then turn down to medium heat and leave it to simmer. When the liquid has reduced by 20%, strain the mixture into two cups and stir in the honey and lemon until you get it just how you like it.

Skin Soothing *Calendula Lotion*

Whether you are having problems with dry, flaky skin or you just feel like pampering yourself, this rich, buttery lotion will leave your skin feeling soft, smooth, and loved. When we care for our skin, there are far-reaching benefits; we feel better about ourselves, our mental health improves, stress levels lower, and we feel more relaxed. So you've no excuse not to find a little "me time" for this lotion in your daily routine.

You will need:

- 2 oz of organic calendula-infused oil
- 3 oz of organic shea butter

Firstly, you'll have to warm the shea butter until it is melted. Pop it in a glass bowl over a pot of boiling water, stirring frequently to make sure the heat is evenly distributed. When it's completely liquid, take it off the heat and stir in the calendula-infused oil. Let the mixture cool down at room temperature for half an hour, and then move it to the refrigerator for another half an hour.

Whip the mixture using a hand mixer for five minutes until the color has turned from yellow to a light cream. The whole thing should look like mayonnaise but smell much better. Transfer it into a sterilized glass jar and store it somewhere dry.

If you want, you can make your own calendula-infused oil. Here's how:

Add a cup of extra virgin olive oil to a mason jar and top off with ½ a cup of dried calendula petals. Cover the top of the jar, but make sure it isn't airtight, or your jar could explode. Put your mason jar inside a large stockpot and add water until it is ⅔ submerged. Bring the water around the jar to a boil and then leave it to simmer for four hours, periodically removing the jar lid and agitating the contents with a skewer or the handle of a spoon. When your oil has cooled slightly, strain it through a fine mesh to remove the dried petals, and then store it in a cool, dark place.

Royal Purple Crown Smoothie

Divine inspiration calls for divine tribute, and nothing is more gorgeous and fitting than the deep violet color of this smoothie—except maybe its taste. Your crown chakra feeds on fruits that share the color of its vibrational energy, and this delicious drink marks a great way to start the day by opening your chakra to the full force of the universe. This recipe makes enough for one large smoothie or two smaller smoothie shots.

You will need:

- 1 banana, frozen in slices
- 1 cup of purple cabbage, grated
- ⅓ cup of blackberries, frozen
- ⅓ cup of blueberries, frozen
- 5 tulsi leaves
- 1 cup plant- or nut-based milk

Put everything into a blender or smoothie maker except for the milk. Give it a quick blitz for 30 seconds, then pour in some of the milk. Keep alternating between blending the mixture and topping up with more milk until you reach the consistency you like best. I prefer my smoothies to be more liquid, so I will use all the milk, but if you like a thicker texture, you might only use half.

CROWN CHAKRA MEDITATION

The herbs bacopa and gotu kola have been used as a traditional meditation aid for thousands of years, and you can add them to this routine to improve your focus as you try to open your crown chakra and receive the wisdom of the universe. You can either brew them into a simple tea, take a few drops of tincture or even chew the edible leaves raw.

Find a quiet spot and settle yourself on the floor, sitting up tall with your head stacked over your spine and your pelvis neutral. Take a deep breath in and draw your shoulders up to your ears. Relax them on the exhale, making sure you release the tension from your shoulders, neck, and jaw.

Close your eyes and imagine an indigo or white ray of light that starts at the top of your head and reaches up toward the stars. As you breathe out, notice how the light flows upward, taking with it your good intentions, positive energy, and spiritual thoughts. When you inhale, imagine the light changing direction and flowing downward, filling you with the love and divine energy that is gifted by the universe. If any other thoughts intrude on your meditation, imagine breathing them out, not through this spiritual light, but through your nose (or mouth) instead. Continue for as long as you feel comfortable.

As you prepare to finish the meditation, on your final exhalation, offer up your thanks to the divine spirits and the universe for accepting you into their world. There is no syllable to chant for your crown chakra. Instead, spend an extra minute sitting quietly, just listening to the world around you. Focus on the sounds you can hear that are far away, then slowly bring your focus closer and closer until the sounds are in the room with you. Then open your eyes.

❦ 8 ❦
HERBAL TEAS: MASTERING THE ART OF THE APOTHECARY AT HOME

Y ou will have noticed that, throughout these chapters, I have included a number of recipes for herbal teas, and there are several reasons for this. Usually, to get the strongest benefits from our herbs, we need to extract their chemical essences rather than eating them whole—indeed, many have such a bitter taste that you would struggle to eat enough to get any benefit at all. There are several ways to do this, including making tinctures, decoctions, and essential oils, but these can take hours, days, and even weeks before they are at their full potency. Steeping the herbs in either hot or cold water offers the fastest way to extract their beneficial properties.

Another good reason to start drinking herbs is that water helps your body absorb them. As the tea makes its way through your digestive system, it is naturally diffused and absorbed like any other food or drink. Your stomach and intestines will automatically regulate your intake, just like they do with the vitamins and minerals extracted from your daily meals. This is because your body doesn't treat the tea like a capsule supplement; it treats it like a natural part of your diet.

I have also mentioned teas a lot because they are a great way for starting herbalists to navigate the thousands of useful herbs. You can buy herbal tea bags that are ready-made, with the right dose and either single herbs or a blend that is professionally designed to work in harmony. Once you have discovered the benefits of herbal teas, you can move on with the confidence to create your own using packets of dried herbs. Finally, if you want to be fully spiritually aligned with your herbs of choice, you can harvest and dry herbs from your own garden, balcony, or yard.

HOW TO DRY HERBS FOR TEA

Making tea from herbs that you have grown yourself is not only immensely satisfying; they may work much better for you on a spiritual level. Remember, all plants have their own spirits, and they will tune into your spiritual energy if you spend time with them, nurture them, and build a relationship. Other herbs will be attuned to you because of a shared ancestral history; for example, many herbs that have traditionally been used in Native American herbalist practices are believed by many to be more efficient for the descendants of the same tribe than they will for practitioners in other parts of the world. This is why, even though regional herbalist recipes are becoming more popular today, we might want to choose herbs that most strongly align with our own spiritual path. So, if given a choice between several herbs that have similar effects, you may want to consider choosing those that mimic your own heritage.

DIY DRYING RACK

If you are going to be drying a large volume of herbs, you should make yourself a drying rack. This can be as simple as a large picture frame with the glass and backing removed. Staple a sheet of cheesecloth or muslin over the frame so that it is taut. You can make several trays and hang them in a stack, using string or chains, or fix blocks of wood to each corner as feet to make them stackable. Keep them somewhere warm and dry, like the kitchen or laundry room, and fill them with herbs as you harvest them. The cloth base will allow air to circulate, drying your herbs from all sides, but it will still take roughly a week to dry your herbs fully, depending on their size. Leaves will usually take less time, but whole flowers, roots, and rhizomes will take the longest.

HARVESTING Your Herbs

When you pick herbs from your own garden, you know that you haven't used any chemicals or pesticides on them. Be careful when wildcrafting, and make sure you wash everything thoroughly, or you might find yourself ingesting something unappetizing and potentially poisonous. Soak your wildcrafted and foraged herbs in a solution of 10% salt water for 20 minutes, and then rinse thoroughly and dry by pressing between sheets of paper towels. This should remove any chemicals, including pesticides and fertilizers. Alternatively, if drying the whole herb, you can tie the stalks into small bunches and hang them upside down from a clothes hanger or a hook.

Every herb utilizes different parts medicinally. For some, like calendula and hibiscus, it is just the flower heads and bases that are used. For others, including ginger and marshmallow, it is the roots, but yet more, like bacopa and fennel, make use of the entire plant. You need to ensure you only dry and use the parts of the plant that are beneficial, especially as there are sometimes compounds in the left-overs that could become toxic in high doses. Until you become more practiced, it's important to keep a herbal guide handy.

Once your herbs have dried, you should be able to remove all leaves and flower heads from the stalks. Crush the leaves and flower heads with a pestle and mortar, and break or chop the stalks into smaller pieces. You can store your dried herbs in sterilized mason jars or in ziplock bags. Don't forget to label them because once you have twenty or so bags of dried herbs in your cabinet, they all start to look very similar.

STRAINING

Because you're going to be brewing with loose-leaf herbal tea—which means it's not contained nicely in a little bag—you will need a few extra bits and pieces in your kitchen drawer. Firstly, it's vital to have something to strain your tea with. You can buy single-cup tea strainers that act like a reusable tea bag: You put the dried herbs inside and drop it into your cup of boiling water. You can also get pots with built-in strainers inside the spout, so you can drop your herbs into the pot and pour out a perfectly clear cup of tea, time after time. If you're going to make larger batches of tea, maybe for iced pitchers or to drink over a few days, it's probably worth investing in a large strainer that you can pour.

BREWING METHODS

How you brew your tea is going to depend on a couple of factors.

- Infusion: If you're using the flowers, leaves, and stems of the herb, you can use this gentle method to extract the flavor and beneficial qualities of the tea. Spoon 1 tsp of your herb into a tea strainer or loose into a cup. If you're making tea in a pot, add 1 tbsp for each cup you'll make. Pour boiling water into the cup, pop a coaster over the top to keep the heat in, and let your herb steep for 10 minutes. Either remove the tea strainer or strain the mixture into another cup and enjoy.
- Concoction: This method works for teas made from the harder parts of your herb, like the root,

bark, rhizomes, or seeds. First, you need to slice your herb into small pieces and then drop it into a saucepan. Add cold water and bring the saucepan of water to a boil—use 1 ½ cups of water and 1 tbsp for each cup of tea you plan to make. Cover the pan and leave it to simmer for at least an hour. Pour through a fine mesh strainer into your favorite cup and enjoy.

- Cold brew: This is a more gentle infusion where you steep the herbs for longer but without the help of boiling water to extract the medicinal compounds from the tea. However, it produces a sweeter tea because the hot water causes the leaves to excrete tannins that have a bitter taste. If you intend to drink your tea cold or don't like adding honey or sugar, then this method will probably work best for you. Fill a jug with cold water and herbs, roughly 2 cups of water to each tablespoon of herbs. Place the jug in the refrigerator and leave overnight or for at least 12 hours. You can leave the herbs in the jug and pour them through a strainer as needed.

HERBAL TEA BLENDS

The beauty of herbal teas is that you can combine any herbs together to suit your purpose. Some people like to design their teas based on their colors, similar flavors, or what parts of the body they want to target. Combining herbs that are tonics with herbs that are healing will create an all-around wonder tea for an organ or an emotion, whereas matching tonic herbs for different parts of the body will give you a tea that works as a complete pick-me-up.

If you are just beginning your journey with herbal teas, you might want to start with single-herb teas. These are called simples and can easily be found in stores or made yourself. A nice simple to start with is peppermint tea, as it doesn't have a bitter flavor, and it is a good all-rounder. Peppermint is often added to other tea blends as a sweetener, but it is absolutely divine on its own. Another good option is cranberry—a tart, fruity tea that relieves stress and cleanses your kidneys.

The advantage of simples is that you can tell whether the herb is working for you or not. If you take a blend with five different herbs, and it makes you feel better, you won't easily know which of the herbs you found an affinity with. For spiritual herbalists, this poses a conundrum, and you'll just have to continue to experiment with different combinations, making notes of what does and doesn't work, using trial and error to find your spirit herbs. It's also worth bearing in mind that the volume of each herb is reduced as others are added because your portion of tea will always be around 1 tbsp, whether that is made up of one herb or ten. You will need to drink more cups of a blend containing peppermint to get the same effect as a simple peppermint tea. Here are some of my favorite chakra tea blends for you to enjoy.

. . .

DANDELION ICED TEA—ROOT Chakra

- 8 whole dandelions, including the root
- 2 bags of black tea
- 1 tsp of grated ginger
- ½ lemon, slices
- ⅓ of a cup of raw honey
- 1 cup of water
- 3 cups of ice

Put the dandelions, ginger, and tea in a saucepan with a cup of water and leave it to simmer for five minutes. Allow it to cool, adding the honey and lemon slices once it is luke-warm. Pop the ice into a bottle or a pitcher and strain the tea over the top. This recipe makes four cups of iced tea and will keep in an airtight container in the refrigerator for one week.

Lady Love Tea—Sacral Chakra

- 1 tbsp dried rose petals
- 1 tsp hibiscus flowers
- 1 tsp crushed chasteberry
- 1 tsp crushed star anise
- 1 tsp cinnamon
- 1 tsp honey or maple syrup
- 4 cups of water

This tonic is believed to alleviate the symptoms of PMS and menopause. Simply add all the herbs to a pan and bring to a boil, then turn down the heat and simmer for 10 minutes. Strain and serve, adding the honey or syrup to taste. This recipe makes two cups and can be reheated later.

Tummy Tonic—Solar Plexus Chakra

- 1 tsp peppermint
- 1 tsp dried raspberry
- 1 tsp licorice root
- ½ tsp dried pineapple
- 2 ½ cups of water

Boil the water and add the licorice root, peppermint, raspberry, and pineapple. Cover the pan and let it simmer for 10 minutes. Pour through a strainer and serve. This recipe makes two cups and can be reheated later. It is a soothing remedy for digestive discomfort, as well as being a restorative tonic over long-term use.

Rose Among (Haw)Thorns Brew—Heart Chakra

- 1 tbsp of dried hawthorn berries
- 1 tbsp of dried rose petals
- 2 cups of boiled water

This bright red blend will open your heart and help to mend a broken one. It's also an amazing tonic for the blood. Steep the herbs in a teapot with the boiled water and leave overnight. When you are ready to drink, strain the tea and reheat it. This recipe makes two cups.

BREATHE SMOOTH BLEND—THROAT Chakra

- 2 tsp marshmallow
- 1 tsp elder
- 1 tsp peppermint
- 1 tsp mullein
- 1 tsp thyme

This blend is best drunk hot to enhance the clearing nature of the herbs, which are designed to unblock sinuses and calm any irritation in your lungs. Put all the herbs into a pot and add 3 cups of boiling water. Allow the herbs to steep for 10-15 minutes, then strain into a cup. Reheat and enjoy. This recipe makes two or three cups.

SEEKING CLARI-TEA—THIRD Eye Chakra

- 2 tsp of mugwort
- 1 tsp of eyebright powder
- 1 tsp of dried lavender flowers
- Honey to taste

Steep the dried mugwort and lavender in a pot with 2 cups of boiled water. After two minutes, stir in the powdered eyebright and as much honey as you like. After two more minutes, strain the tea into a cup and enjoy. This blend will open your third eye chakra and help you to see the truth around you.

Pathway to Enlightenment Blend—Crown Chakra

- 4 tbsp of gotu kola powder
- 4 tbsp of peppermint
- 2 tbsp of fresh rosemary
- 8 cups of boiling water

Place the herbs in a large pan with a lid and pour over the boiling water. Close the lid and leave the infusion to steep for half an hour. Strain into a pitcher or jug and pour out a cup when you feel the need for a brainpower boost or to reconnect with the spiritual plane. This recipe makes 8 cups and will keep in the refrigerator in an airtight container for a week. Reheat as necessary.

THE BEST FLOWERS FOR TEA

Growing flowering herbs in your garden can be doubly beneficial: Not only will you have a ready supply of flowers for your brew, but you will get the mental health benefits of enjoying the beauty they bring to any space. The following flowers, on top of those mentioned in earlier chapters, make especially lovely simple teas or can be combined to make starter blends.

Borage

These pretty blue star-shaped flowers add a little bit of glamor to every tea garden. Not only is borage a key tonic for your kidneys, but it also lifts your spirits and gives you the courage to keep fighting, even when the present seems a little dark. Use fresh leaves, flowers, and seeds in a cold brew and drink with ice.

Catnip

A well-known herb for your feline companion, catnip doesn't save all its tricks for the cats. Dry the flowers and leaves and brew them in a hot infusion to help with the symptoms of PMS, acid reflux, and insomnia. This versatile herb also acts as a calming agent for days when you find it difficult to relax and your anxiety is disrupting your digestion.

Feverfew

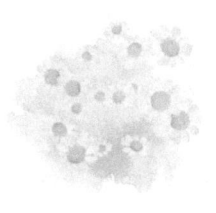

A member of the daisy family, this herb has small, yellow flowers, slightly fluffy leaves, and hairy stems, all of which can be used for making tea. It should be brewed as a hot infusion and is a wonderful cure for allergies like hay fever because it is a natural antihistamine. Drink a cup every morning to relieve the symptoms and set yourself up for an allergy-free day. It is also an effective tonic to help you recover from a headache or migraine, and if drunk regularly, it may prevent them from reoccurring.

Hops

Usually found in beer, this dark green vine produces flowers that look like small pine cones. They can be harvested, dried, and brewed in a hot infusion to help send you off to sleep. Hops have a long list of positive effects on women because they are full of plant estrogens, and so this plant is used to treat PMS, menopausal symptoms, IBS, and nervous anxiety. If you inhale the steam from your hops tea, it will help to clear mucus from your lungs.

LEMON VERBENA

This shrub looks and smells great in any garden. Its pale green leaves contrast nicely with its purple flowers, both of which are dried for tea making. Often added to other herbs to improve their flavor, lemon verbena has its own benefits that shouldn't be ignored: It has a sedative effect on the stomach, relieving gas and cramps, and it also beautifies the skin. Brew as a hot infusion for a delicious after-dinner drink.

MEADOWSWEET

A favorite herb of European druids, these cream-colored flowers give off an almond-like scent. A natural pain reliever, meadowsweet tea, made of the leaves and flowers, also calms and soothes your stomach. This herb is restorative, protecting the lining of your stomach and intestines, and regular use will keep your digestive system in optimum health.

PASSIONFLOWER

These exotic purple flowers come from the West Indies and grow on trailing vines that thrive in the sunlight. When taken as a tea, passionflower is used to treat nervous conditions and brings the best benefits when it is part of a daily or weekly routine. If you're feeling irritable, anxious, stressed, or suffering from tension headaches and nervous exhaustion, this is the tonic for you. It is also a mild sedative and mood lifter, good for raising your spirits and helping you to see the light. Brew the flowers in a hot infusion and add lavender for an added sleep booster.

ST. John's Wort

Traditionally viewed as a purifier and healer, there are very few conditions that can't be helped by a hot infusion of St. John's Wort. The delicate yellow flowers are full of volatile oil that can be extracted during the infusion process. This herb is a marvelous tonic for the nervous system and will repair the damage done by

prolonged periods of exhaustion and stress. It also eases symptoms of depression if drunk regularly.

Wood Betony

Clusters of purple flowers crowd around the top of stalks and give wood betony its unmistakable appearance. It used to be known as bishopswort and was thought to signify sanctity. Dry the whole plant while flowering to capture the best of its healing power, then brew as a hot infusion for a number of uses. Drinking wood betony tea can help to clear brain fog and headaches, and you can also use it to soothe cuts and scrapes, sores, and infections.

Yarrow

Yarrow stalks grow tall and proud, erupting in clustered heads of flowers throughout the summer months. A common meadow wildflower, it has been used as a healing herb for thousands of years. You

can dry the whole plant when it is in full bloom and use it as an infusion. Yarrow tea should be your go-to tea for fighting colds and the flu, so brew it as hot as you can to sweat out the virus. Once the tea has cooled, you can use it externally to speed up the healing of wounds, burns, and ulcers.

Sun	Mon	Tue	Wed	Thu	Fri	Sat
			1	2	3	4
12	13	14	15	16	17	18
19	20	21	22	23	24	25
26	27	28	29	30	31	

January

9

YOUR SPIRITUAL HERBALISM ROUTINE: A 14-DAY PLAN TO REALIGN AND REJUVENATE YOUR CHAKRAS USING HERBS

Hopefully, as you read through the pages of this book, there are certain herbs that will have reached out to you and have stuck in your mind. Whether this comes from gut instinct that draws you towards them or your brain telling you they match your needs, you will always want to listen to your body. It will be interpreting messages that you cannot comprehend and working to guide you toward the herbs that feed and nourish your spirit.

I spoke briefly in the introduction about the importance of establishing herbs as part of your daily routine and using rituals that give you time to ruminate on your connection with nature. In the rest of this chapter, you will find a 14-day plan suggesting ways in which you can use the herbs, recipes, and meditations presented in this guide to enrich your life on a regular basis. The plan is here to be used as you see fit: follow it religiously for two weeks and then make some personal adjustments, or chop and change it around to suit your existing routines. For example, you might already use a facial toner at bedtime, but now you might want to change it to a herb that is better suited to you.

One important point to mention is that not all herbs will give you an immediate result. Some take at least six weeks to build up in your system, and it is only after this time that you will notice their effect. If you aren't sure whether a herb is working for you after this time, you might like to switch it out for something with similar benefits.

In the following plan, I am going to focus on one chakra each day. If you want to craft your own routine in order to pay more attention to a specific chakra, then I would suggest concentrating on it over a number of consecutive days. Also, consider beginning your routine in the phase of the moon that corresponds to that chakra; for example, a three-day routine focusing on cleansing your solar plexus chakra should begin during a waxing moon in order to harness the lunar power of transformation.

WEEK ONE

This routine is going to be split into morning and evening rituals, but you can, of course, find time at any point to nourish your spiritual self. Do not feel that you need to follow each day to the letter—unless you want to—but feel free to pick and choose from the activities. If journaling isn't for you, or you have no crystals to hand, you will still gain plenty of benefits from the rest of the routine.

MONDAY

Chakra focus: The root chakra

- **Morning:** Rehydration should be the first thing on your mind in the morning. While you have been asleep, your body has dipped into its fluid reserves, and replenishing them is one of the best ways to wake up your brain. While many people traditionally turn to coffee for their morning brew, it isn't as hydrating as tea. Fill a water bottle with Dandelion Iced Tea and leave it by your bedside, so you can enjoy it as part of your morning wake-up ritual. While you sip it, the beginning of the week is a great time for journaling. Write down your thoughts and intentions for the week; is there anything coming up that is worrying you or anything you are particularly looking forward to?

- **Evening:** Enjoy a bowl of Warming Root Chakra Soup. Cooking for the chakras is a great way of revitalizing them and incorporating them into your existing routines. Before bed, take five minutes to ground yourself with some yoga poses. Your root chakra can be realigned with grounded balances like mountain pose and tree pose. Finish with a root chakra meditation.

TUESDAY

Chakra focus: The sacral chakra

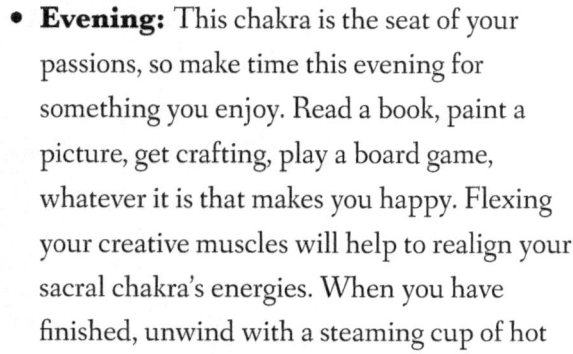

- **Morning:** Before getting out of bed, take some orange crystals and place them over your sacral chakra. I recommend carnelian, sunstone, or orange calcite. Focus your intentions for the day through the stones and into your sacral chakra. Once you are awake, blitz yourself a Sacral Boost Smoothie. This will give you a good boost of fiber and slow-release carbs to see you through the morning.

- **Evening:** This chakra is the seat of your passions, so make time this evening for something you enjoy. Read a book, paint a picture, get crafting, play a board game, whatever it is that makes you happy. Flexing your creative muscles will help to realign your sacral chakra's energies. When you have finished, unwind with a steaming cup of hot cocoa. Stir squares of dark chocolate into hot milk and add a couple of cinnamon sticks for flavor and as a tonic for your circulatory system.

WEDNESDAY

Chakra focus: The solar plexus chakra

- **Morning:** Lots of people meditate at the end of the day as a way to clear the mind before bed, but meditating first thing in the morning when your mind is still empty can help you achieve a greater state of relaxation and bring you closer to your spiritual self. Use this time to listen to the world around you as you perform your solar plexus chakra meditation. Finish off with a cup of Antioxidant Tea to warm and revitalize your liver.

- **Evening:** Have a cup of Tummy Tonic after dinner to aid digestion and prevent any irritations affecting your sleep. Light some candles to appeal to your chakra's fire element, and run yourself a Calming Camomile Oat Bath. Now is also a good time to revisit your journal from Monday. How are your thoughts and intentions for the week coming to fruition? Your solar plexus chakra contains the essence of your self-image, so now is a good time to journal some personal reflections. How can you grow and move towards your personal goals? Set yourself a positive target for the week—this could be to try a new exercise class, eat something healthy, or work on a new skill for work.

THURSDAY

Chakra focus: The heart chakra

- **Morning:** To realign the heart chakra, we're going to focus on opening yourself to giving and receiving love. Use your journal to write a message to a friend, lover, or family member, expressing your true feelings for them. Be open and honest, looking deep inside your heart to find your innermost emotions. If you choose someone you have recently had a falling out with, take this opportunity to forgive them. To take advantage of this chakra's elemental alignment with air, you can do your journaling outside or near an open window. Take a spoonful of Heart Happiness Boosting Syrup before you write for a clearer focus on your intentions.

- **Evening:** Spend time this evening with a loved one or a family pet. Talk on the phone with someone you haven't seen for a while. This is your time to bask in the love that other people have for you. Make a batch of The Way to Your Heart Chakra Truffles and either share with a friend or treat yourself. Then, unwind with a eucalyptus shower steam: Hang a bundle of fresh eucalyptus branches over the showerhead to release the soothing essential oils.

FRIDAY

Chakra focus: The throat chakra

- **Morning:** Start the day by rehydrating with a glass of Homemade Elderflower Cordial. The throat chakra is all about communication and expressing yourself, so what better way to end the working

week than by some joyful singing? Make yourself a playlist with your three favorite karaoke songs and belt them out at the top of your voice. Pack yourself a snack of blueberries and blackberries to enjoy when you get peckish.

- **Evening:** Time to give your lungs and airways a rest after a week of work. Make yourself a herbal steam bath with a mixture of sage, elderflower, and thyme. Chuck 1 tbsp of each herb into a mixing bowl, add boiling water, and stir. Place a towel over the bowl and your head, and enjoy your own personal herbal sauna. You can change the herbs to energize different chakras and organs, but this combination is always a good starting point. Treat yourself to a nighttime snack of Superhoney on toasted bread. If you spent a lot of time talking today, recharge your throat chakra's powers of communication by placing some crystals next to your bed: I recommend sodaline, blue calcite, and lapis lazuli.

SATURDAY

Chakra focus: The third eye chakra

- **Morning:** Wake yourself up
  with a (Third) Eye Opening
  Morning Smoothie. Make sure
  you open all the curtains and
  blinds and let the natural
  daylight into your home, as
  light is the element associated
  with restoring this chakra.
  Begin your day with meditation and alternate
  nostril breathing. While you are meditating,
  visualize yourself realizing your dreams and
  sending that manifestation energy out into the
  universe. Find yourself a sunny spot and
  practice some yoga to increase the energy flow
  to your third eye chakra—dolphin pose is good
  for this, as is lotus pose.
- **Evening:** It is good practice to leave a dream
  journal next to your bed so that you can record
  your dreams when you wake up. If you haven't
  got one, now is a good time to get it ready
  because if your third eye chakra is open and
  energized, your dreams will be vivid and
  insightful. Put a Sweet Dreams Pillow Pouch
  inside your pillowcase and pour yourself a
  nighttime cup of Lavender and Chamomile

Bedtime Brew. Make sure you turn off all screens at least an hour before bedtime.

SUNDAY

Chakra focus: The crown chakra

- **Morning:** Reheat a cup of Pathway to Enlightenment Blend and enjoy quiet surroundings. Perform the crown chakra meditation to open up your crown chakra and restore your spiritual connection with the universe. Take a sensory walk around your home to really ground yourself in your reality and your surroundings: Walk barefoot across different floor surfaces, touch the different textures of your furnishings, and listen to the sounds of your footsteps and your breathing. Give thanks to the universe for the bountiful gifts of beauty that are in your life.

- **Evening:** Look back through your journal and see how well you have realized your intentions for the week. Where you faltered, ask the universe to open your eyes to the lesson you can take from it. Take a relaxing bath or shower and pamper your skin by rubbing in Skin Soothing Calendula Lotion to help seal in the moisture and soothe away any dry patches.

WEEK TWO

To focus more deeply on one chakra at a time, you could merge these weeks and observe Monday, Monday, Tuesday, Tuesday, etc. I have deliberately given two distinct weeks to illustrate the variety of chakra-boosting activities to choose from.

MONDAY

Chakra focus: The root chakra

- **Morning:** Get yourself out into nature this morning, preferably somewhere quiet and private, like your backyard, nearby woodland, a park, or the beach. Go as early as you can, so you can fully experience the waking of the world. If you cannot get outside, you can simulate nature sounds through headphones while meditating and imagining yourself outside. Spending time in nature is incredibly important to ground you to the earth and feel our planet's vibrational energy. Disconnection from the earth can leave you feeling adrift and directionless. Try and continue your connection with nature throughout the day by eating your lunch outside.

- **Evening:** Watch the sunset, mentally giving thanks to the universe that you are able to be a part of all creation. If you have crystals, you can hold them and recharge them now, using the energy of the sunset and your spiritual gratefulness: Good root chakra crystals are tiger's eye, hematite, obsidian, and red jasper. After dinner, enjoy a fruity You Can't "Beet" This Chakra Smoothie. Go for a nighttime run if you have somewhere safe to do so.

TUESDAY

Chakra focus: The sacral chakra

- **Morning:** Wake up your sacral chakra with some yoga stretches that use a sacral twist. Revolved triangle pose is a lovely choice as it pulls your energy toward your sacral chakra. Fill your breakfast with orange fruits; mango,  papaya, peaches, and oranges. Top off your morning with a cup of Hibiscus Tea or Lady

Love Tea if you are experiencing menopausal or premenstrual symptoms.

- **Evening:** Continue the day's focus on orange foods with a warming bowl of Supercharge Your Sacral Soup. Your feelings of self-worth are rooted in your sacral chakra, and when it is blocked, it can be difficult to see your own value. Use this time with your journal to write out five ways you add value to the world. Think about your relationships with others and how your actions have made positive changes, and celebrate any successes, no matter how small. If you have done this step before, flip back through your book and remind yourself of what you wrote on previous occasions.

WEDNESDAY

Chakra focus: The solar plexus chakra

- Morning: Get yourself off to a good start with a breakfast of Energy Boosting Solar Plexus Smoothie. This chakra is aligned with the sun, so some yoga sun salutations will help to get your energy flowing in the right direction. Finish off your workout with Boat Pose to really center your energy at your solar plexus. Try and spend as much time as possible today soaking in the sunlight—wearing adequate clothing and sunscreen, of course. Even if it's a cloudy day, you will benefit from the natural light.

- **Evening:** Buy yourself a bunch of bright yellow flowers to bring positive energy into your home. Daffodils, tulips, sunflowers, and roses will all spark joy every time you see them. Surround them with yellow tourmaline, calcite, and citrine crystals to soak up their playful, harmonious vibes. Enjoy a cup of Immune Boosting Astragalus Tea—or just make a simple tea from Astragalus root—drunk next to your flowers.

THURSDAY

Chakra focus: The heart chakra

- **Morning:** Grab your heart-healing crystals and perform your heart chakra meditation. Hold your crystals over your heart chakra for a few more moments and ask your heart

what it wants for the day. Use this intuition's energy to charge up your crystals, then carry them with you all day to help steer the universe in the right direction. Wake yourself up with Peaceful Warrior yoga poses. This pose opens your heart chakra and sends your loving energy out into the world. Finish your workout with a Love Yourself Smoothie.

- **Evening:** This evening's focus is going to be on your lungs and releasing stored grief. We all carry around grief, even if we aren't aware of it, and leaving it to stagnate in your lungs can be problematic. Find yourself a quiet spot to perform the sound healing exercise. A good rule of thumb is one cleansing exhale to four recharging inhalations, repeated as often as you feel necessary. Releasing grief can sap your energy, so finish off with a cup of Rose Among (Haw) Thorns Brew and a quiet activity, like watching your favorite movie or reading a gentle novel.

FRIDAY

Chakra focus: The throat chakra

- **Morning:** A well-balanced throat chakra helps you to speak your truth and express your individuality. Use your journal this morning to think about the aspects of your personality that you wish the world saw more of. Think about the ways you can express yourself better; through your actions, your clothes, and your hobbies. If you like, you could draw your personality rather than write about it. Have a cup of Breathe Easy Blend to recharge your throat chakra for a day of communicating.

- **Evening:** Now is a good time to clear your home of any residual negative energy by smudging. You can use sage, white sage, sweet grass, or lavender. Once you have cleared the space, you can invite positive energy to take up residence instead. Perform your throat chakra meditation and try some rhythmic chanting. After dinner, enjoy a glass of Banish Those Blues Smoothie, especially if you've eaten something spicy, as this will cool and restore your throat tissue.

SATURDAY

Chakra focus: The third eye chakra

- **Morning:** Before going to bed the night before, turn off your alarm and leave your curtains or blinds open. This morning, you are going to wake up with the steadily increasing natural sunlight. This is extremely energizing for your pineal gland. Before getting out of bed, place your favorite third eye chakra stone between your eyebrows—over the spot where your chakra resides—and imagine it drawing energy into your chakra. Stones I recommend are amethyst, azurite, and quartz. Speak out loud some of the following affirmations to charge your stones and chakra with positive intentions:

My mind is healthy and full of wisdom
My imagination is creative and free-flowing
My intuition is trustworthy, and I follow it willingly
My spirit is alive with the truth of my soul
My eyes are open to the lessons of the universe

- **Evening:** Make a commitment to spend this evening without blue-light-producing screens and keep synthetic light levels to a minimum in order to keep your third eye chakra regulating your sleep patterns. As the sun goes down, enjoy a warming cup or two of Seeking Clari-tea and choose an activity that feeds your brain: a crossword puzzle, board game, learning a new skill, or researching something that interests you. Stimulating your brain will help to keep it healthy and vital.

SUNDAY

Chakra focus: The crown chakra

- **Morning:** While your other chakras have foods that nourish them, your crown chakra is only nourished by spiritual means, so it is actually associated with fasting. Today, plan for an intermittent fast, where you only eat between 10 am and 6 pm. If you have long-term health conditions, like diabetes, IBS, or cancer, or are taking medication, please consult your healthcare professional before attempting to fast for any period of time. Herbal teas will not break your fast, so whip up a batch of Tempting Tulsi Tea to get you through the morning.

- **Evening:** For your evening meal, choose foods that are white or indigo, like an eggplant risotto, and finish off with a Royal Purple Crown Smoothie. This is a good day to tend to any herbs and plants you are growing, taking the time to talk to them, feed them, and thank them for the beauty and healing qualities they bring. Finish your evening with a crown chakra meditation and enjoy the peace and stillness of the night. You might like to sit outside and contemplate the stars above if you can see them. Observe the vastness of the universe, how it is eternal and never-ending, and you are blessed to be a part of it.

AFTERWORD

The aim of this book is to guide you on your way as you take those first tentative steps along the path of spiritual herbalism, arming you with bouquets of recipes, meditations, and botanical revelations along the way. Your journey began when you made the decision to turn the first page, and now that you have made it to the end, it is in no way over. You have the tools and the wisdom to begin making changes to your life that will take you to places of such positive energy and spiritual fulfillment that many people dream of reaching.

I said at the start that these pages would bring education and enlightenment, but that is only because you have opened your heart and mind to the possibility of personal and spiritual growth. Finding the right balance is never easy —otherwise, everyone would be perfectly aligned all the time—and it is something that can change from day to day.

Life will often challenge you, and this has the potential to push you away from your true spiritual path, perhaps making you feel stressed, anxious, and untrusting of your own instincts. This is exactly where spiritual herbalism can help you, and I congratulate your intuition for leading you on this path.

You have now had a chance to learn about more than 25 important herbs and how they can help to cleanse, revitalize, and support your entire body. Not only that, but you now also know how to use them to reconnect with your spiritual self and open the gateway to the spiritual plane, where you can communicate with the divine energy of the universe.

My advice is to find ways to incorporate spiritual herbalism into your life in a way that works for you. Trust your heart intuition and your gut feelings; I bet they have already spoken to you and let you know which herbs to try first. You may enjoy growing them yourself or decide that your energy is better spent elsewhere and instead find some amazing suppliers for dried herbs and tea blends.

As you work to rebuild and realign your chakras, you are going to experience so many positive changes in your life. I wholeheartedly suggest keeping a journal, so you can look back in the future and marvel at how far you have come. As you add more and more spiritual rituals and practices to your daily routine, you will experiment with new ways to augment them with your growing knowledge of herbalism. From teas and tinctures to essential oils, herbal steams, smoothies, soups, and salads, there are many ways in which our plant allies can benefit us. I hope you enjoy experimenting with different herbal tea blends and find pleasure in wildcrafting and harvesting your own herbs. There is something innately satisfying in making your own herbal medicines. I like to think it is our ancestral memories coming to the surface.

Where can you go from here? You now have knowledge of some of the basics of herbalism and how they can work for you, but there are thousands of other secrets still to be uncovered. Start by working with the herbs and recipes in this book, as they are some of the most effective and universally accepted. If you want to delve deeper into the realms of herbal healing, there are a number of wonderful websites that offer structured courses and detailed herbal encyclopedias where you can find cures and tonics for almost everything. You can search for the herbs you think are most aligned with your spirit, or you can research the plants you find growing around you. The world of spiritual herbalism is vast and full of knowledgeable practitioners who are willing to share their wisdom.

Finally, remember that spiritual herbalism is about more than just what these herbs can do for your body. The plant spirits and the energy from Mother Nature herself will also act as tonics for your own spirit. Our plant allies want to help us and heal us, and you will always want to repay them with gratitude. Be mindful of taking more than you need, and be kind enough to remember to leave enough for the next person.

I hope that incorporating spiritual herbalism into your

life brings you joy, positivity, and a renewed connection with the greater universal intelligence.

REFERENCES

Ajmera, R. (2017). 8 Benefits of Hibiscus Tea. Healthline.
https://www.healthline.com/nutrition/hibiscus-tea-benefits

Anima Mundi Herbals. (n.d.). THE ASTROLOGY OF Herbs.
https://animamundiherbals.com/blogs/blog/the-astrology-of-herbs

Anon. (n.d.). Ginger-fennel-peppermint Tonic Recipe. Group Recipes.
http://www.grouprecipes.com/64111/ginger-fennel-peppermint-tonic.html

Apni Kheti. (n.d.). Shankhpushpi Farming Punjab. https://www.ap-nikheti.com/en/pn/agriculture/horticulture/medicinal-plants/shankhpushpi

Balogh, A. (2019). Caring for Roses: A Beginner's Rose Growing Guide - Garden Design. GardenDesign.com. https://www.gardende-sign.com/roses/care.html

Banyan Botanicals. (n.d.-a). Ginger: Getting to Know Your Herbal Allies. https://www.banyanbotanicals.com/info/blog-the-banyan-insight/details/getting-to-know-your-herbal-allies-ginger/

Banyan Botanicals. (n.d.-b). The Benefits of Hibiscus. https://www.banyanbotanicals.com/info/plants/ayurvedic-herbs/the-benefits-of-hibiscus/

Banyan Botanicals. (n.d.-c). The Benefits of Shatavari. https://www.banyanbotanicals.com/info/plants/ayurvedic-herbs/shatavari/

BBC Gardeners World Magazine. (n.d.). Ocimum tenuiflorum. https://www.gardenersworld.com/plants/ocimum-tenuiflorum/

Blankespoor, J. (2012, December 13). Lavender's Medicinal and Aromatherapy Uses | Chestnut School of Herbal Medicine. Chestnut School of Herbal Medicine. https://chestnutherbs.com/lavenders-medicinal-and-aromatherapy-uses-and-lavender-truffles/

Blankespoor, J. (2022, May 26). Calendula, An Edible & Medicinal Flower | How to Use Calendula. Chestnut School of Herbal Medicine.

https://chestnutherbs.com/calendula-sunshine-incarnate-an-edible-and-medicinal-flower/

Bookless, C. (n.d.). Sacral Soup. Conscious Cook. *https://www.conscious-cook.co/recipes/sacral-soup*

Brennan, P. (2019, December 26). Growing Damiana Plants From Seed. Sacred Plant Co. *https://www.sacredplantco.com/post/growing-damiana-plants-from-seed*

Brooks, N. A., Wilcox, G., Walker, K. Z., Ashton, J. F., Cox, M. B., & Stojanovska, L. (2008). Beneficial effects of Lepidium meyenii (Maca) on psychological symptoms and measures of sexual dysfunction in postmenopausal women are not related to estrogen or androgen content. Menopause, 15(6), 1157–1162. *https://doi.org/10.1097/gme.ob013e3181732953*

Buckley, S. (2022, March 21). Refreshing dandelion iced tea recipe. Frolic and Fare. *https://frolicandfare.com/dandelion-root-iced-tea/*

Buckner, H. (2020, April 30). How to Grow and Use Motherwort | Gardener's Path. Gardener's Path. *https://gardenerspath.com/plants/herbs/grow-motherwort/*

Chandran, R. (n.d.). Extension | Mugwort. Extension. *https://extension.wvu.edu/lawn-gardening-pests/weeds/mugwort*

Chauhan, D. M. (2019a, April 22). Shatavari Plant - Shatavari Uses, Benefits and Effects on Dosha. Planet Ayurveda. *https://www.planetayurveda.com/library/shatavari-asparagus-racemosus/*

Chauhan, D. M. (2019b, April 24). Shankhpushpi (Convolvulus Pluricaulis) - Medicinal Properties, Benefits & Dosage. Planet Ayurveda. *https://www.planetayurveda.com/library/shankhpushpi-convolvulus-pluricaulis/*

Cheryls Herbs. (2020, April 13). HERBAL INFORMATION SHEET: BACOPA. *https://cherylsherbs.com/blogs/herb-profile-directory/herbal-information-sheet-bacopa*

Chow, M. (2023, February 5). Botanica Erotica: Exploring Sensuality and Aphrodisiac Herbs. Birth Song Botanicals Co. *https://www.birthsongbotanicals.com/blogs/birth-song-blog/aphrodisiac-herbs*

Christiansen, S. (2019, September 5). The Health Benefits of Mugwort. Verywell Health. *https://www.verywellhealth.com/mugwort-benefits-side-effects-dosage-and-interactions-4767226*

College of Naturopathic Medicine. (2020, May 22). How to Remove

Pesticides From Your Produce. https://www.naturopathy-uk.com/news/news-cnm-blog/blog/2020/05/22/how-to-remove-pesticides-from-vegetables-and-fruits-2/

Damiana Shrub: Growing, Healing & Magickal Uses. (2019, November 2). Magickalspot.com. https://magickalspot.com/damiana/

de la Foret, R. (n.d.). The Marshmallow Herb. Herbs with Rosalee. https://www.herbalremediesadvice.org/marshmallow-herb.html

Dehnke, A. (2021, June 11). A Beginner's Guide to the Chakras. Yoga Journal. https://www.yogajournal.com/practice/yoga-sequences-level/beginners-guide-chakras/

Dessinger, H. (2022, February 20). DIY Liver Love Detox Support Tincture Recipe. Mommypotamus. https://mommypotamus.com/liver-tincture-recipe/

Doctor NDTV. (n.d.). Avoid Ginger If You Are Dealing With Any Of These Health Conditions. https://doctor.ndtv.com/living-healthy/avoid-ginger-if-you-are-dealing-with-any-of-these-health-conditions-1779507

Doyle, E. (2022a, August 3). Motherwort: The Lion Hearted Herb. The School of Evolutionary Herbalism. https://www.evolutionaryherbalism.com/2022/08/03/motherwort-the-lion-hearted-herb/

Doyle, E. (2022b, December 7). Mugwort: The Herb of Dreams. The School of Evolutionary Herbalism. https://www.evolutionaryherbalism.com/2022/12/07/mugwort-the-herb-of-dreams/

Dyer, M. H. (2022, July 27). StackPath. Gardening Know How. https://www.gardeningknowhow.com/ornamental/groundcover/gotu-kola/gotu-kola-information.htm

Eisler, M. (2015, November 4). Nadi Shodhana: How to Practice Alternate Nostril Breathing. Chopra. https://chopra.com/articles/nadi-shodhana-how-to-practice-alternate-nostril-breathing

Euphoric Herbals. (n.d.). 11 Herbs for Brain Health, Mental Energy, & Focus. Euphoric Herbals. https://www.euphoricherbals.com/blogs/news/11-herbs-for-brain-health-mental-energy-focus

Floranella. (2017, January 1). Elder Berry and Elder Flower in Herbalism and Aromatherapy. https://www.floranella.com/sample-lessons/elder-berry-and-elder-flower

Foley, M. (2018, April 17). 5 Herbs to Open Your Third Eye. The Alchemist's Kitchen. https://wisdom.thealchemistskitchen.com/5-herbs-to-open-your-third-eye/

Fowler, A. (2021, June 12). *How to grow native red clover*. The Guardian. https://www.theguardian.com/lifeand-style/2021/jun/12/how-to-grow-native-red-clover

Freed, M. (2017, June 20). *Hawthorn: Heart Healing from Physical to Spiritual*. Traditional Roots Institute. https://traditionalroots.org/hawthorn-heart-healing-from-physical-to-spiritual/

Gaia Herbs. (n.d.-a). *Bacopa*. Retrieved March 28, 2023, from https://www.gaiaherbs.com/blogs/herbs/bacopa

Gaia Herbs. (n.d.-b). *Eucalyptus*. https://www.gaiaherbs.com/blogs/herbs/eucalyptus

Gaia Herbs. (n.d.-c). *The 5 Best Herbs for Fertility and Reproductive Health*. Gaia Herbs. https://www.gaiaherbs.com/blogs/seeds-of-knowledge/herbs-for-fertility

Gardeners World. (n.d.). *Foeniculum vulgare*. https://www.gardenersworld.com/plants/foeniculum-vulgare/

Golden Poppy. (2017, May 31). *Working With The Crown Chakra*. https://goldenpoppyherbs.com/working-with-the-crown-chakra/

Golden Poppy Herbs. (2017a, January 15). *Working With The Heart Chakra*. https://goldenpoppyherbs.com/working-with-the-heart-chakra/

Golden Poppy Herbs. (2017b, February 2). *Working With The Throat Chakra*. https://goldenpoppyherbs.com/working-with-the-throat-chakra/

Gonzales, G. F. (2012). *Ethnobiology and Ethnopharmacology ofLepidium meyenii(Maca), a Plant from the Peruvian Highlands*. Evidence-Based Complementary and Alternative Medicine, 2012, 1–10. https://doi.org/10.1155/2012/193496

Goodnet. (2020, October 20). *Cleansing Herbs for Each Chakra*. Goodnet. https://www.goodnet.org/articles/cleansing-herbs-for-each-chakra

Grieve, M. (n.d.). *A Modern Herbal*. https://botanical.com/

Grow Tea Company. (n.d.). *How to Cold Brew Tea*. https://www.growtea-company.com/blogs/news/how-to-cold-brew-tea

Hart, K. (2018). *Third Eye Chakra Recipe Book: Improve Perception And Develop Intuition, Activate Psychic Abilities, Trust Gut Feeling, Receive Inner Guidance Using Purple Foods (Kindle Edition)*. Independently published.

Healthline. (2020, March 13). *Mullein Leaf Uses, Benefits & Risks*. https://www.healthline.com/health/mullein-leaf

Heirloom Organics. (n.d.). How to Grow Astragalus. http://www.heirloom-organics.com/guide/va/guidetogrowingastragalus.html

Herb Pharm. (2022, February 2). 13 Nervine Herbs to Support the Nervous System. https://www.herb-pharm.com/blogs/herbal-education/13-nervine-herbs

Herbal Academy. (2015, September 3). Motherwort: The Plant World's Mama Bear. Herbal Academy. https://theherbalacademy.com/motherwort-the-plant-worlds-mama-bear/

Herbal Academy. (2020, March 11). Milk Thistle: A Spring Herb Your Liver Will Love. https://theherbalacademy.com/milk-thistle/

Hocurscak, S. (2014, April 9). Red Clover, Red Clover, Bring Healing on Over - Red Clover Tea Recipe. Herbal Academy. https://theherbalacademy.com/red-clover-tea/

Hopkins Medicine. (n.d.). Ginger Benefits. https://www.hopkinsmedicine.org/health/wellness-and-prevention/ginger-benefits

How to grow ginger. (n.d.). Love the Garden. https://www.lovethegarden.com/uk-en/article/how-grow-ginger

Hudson, T. (n.d.). The Surprising Health Benefits of Hibiscus. Gaia Herbs. Retrieved March 11, 2023, from https://www.gaiaherbs.com/blogs/seeds-of-knowledge/the-surprising-health-benefits-of-hibiscus

Indigo Herbs. (n.d.-a). Damiana Benefits & Information. https://www.indigo-herbs.co.uk/natural-health-guide/benefits/damiana

Indigo Herbs. (n.d.-b). Elecampane Benefits. https://www.indigo-herbs.co.uk/natural-health-guide/benefits/elecampane

Indigo Herbs. (n.d.-c). Eyebright Benefits. https://www.indigo-herbs.co.uk/natural-health-guide/benefits/eyebright

Indigo Herbs. (n.d.-d). Gotu Kola Benefits. https://www.indigo-herbs.co.uk/natural-health-guide/benefits/gotu-kola

Indigo Herbs. (n.d.-e). Tulsi Benefits. Retrieved March 28, 2023, from https://www.indigo-herbs.co.uk/natural-health-guide/benefits/tulsi-holy-basil

Jacob, L. (2023, January 11). What is Mullein? Nutra Tea. https://nutratea.co.uk/what-is-mullein/

Jain, R. (2020a, September 3). Manipura Chakra: Healing Powers of Solar Plexus Chakra. Arhanta Yoga Ashram. https://www.arhantayoga.org/blog/manipura-chakra-healing-powers-of-the-solar-plexus-chakra/

Jain, R. (2020b, October 7). *Ajna Chakra Your Third-Eye Chakra Awakening | Arhanta Yoga Blog.* Arhanta Yoga Ashram. https://www.arhantayoga.org/blog/ajna-chakra-your-third-eye-chakra-awakening/

Jain, R. (2020c, October 8). *Crown Chakra: The Divine Energy of Sahasrara Chakra | Arhanta Blog.* Arhanta Yoga Ashram. https://www.arhantayoga.org/blog/crown-chakra-divine-energy-of-sahasrara-chakra/

Jaiswal, Y. S., & Williams, L. L. (2017). A glimpse of Ayurveda – The forgotten history and principles of Indian traditional medicine. *Journal of Traditional and Complementary Medicine, 7*(1), 50–53. https://doi.org/10.1016/j.jtcme.2016.02.002

Johnson, J. (2016a, May 27). *Tips on Balancing the Root Chakra.* Herbal Academy. https://theherbalacademy.com/tips-on-balancing-the-root-chakra/

Johnson, J. (2016b, June 27). *Tips on Balancing the Sacral Chakra.* Herbal Academy. https://theherbalacademy.com/tips-on-balancing-the-sacral-chakra/

Johnson, J. (2016c, July 22). *Tips On Balancing the Solar Plexus Chakra.* Herbal Academy. https://theherbalacademy.com/tips-on-balancing-the-solar-plexus-chakra/

Johnson, J. (2016d, August 17). *Tips On Balancing The Heart Chakra.* Herbal Academy. https://theherbalacademy.com/tips-balancing-heart-chakra/

Johnson, J. (2016e, September 23). *Tips on Balancing the Throat Chakra.* Herbal Academy. https://theherbalacademy.com/tips-balancing-throat-chakra/

Johnson, J. (2016f, October 17). *How To Balance the Third Eye (or the 6th Chakra).* Herbal Academy. https://theherbalacademy.com/balance-the-third-eye/

Joyful Belly. (n.d.). *Damiana.* https://www.joyfulbelly.com/Ayurveda/product/Damiana/432

Justis, A. (2015, September 17). *A Family Herb: Chamomile Flower.* Herbal Academy. https://theherbalacademy.com/a-family-herb-chamomile-flower/

Justis, A. (2016, May 11). *A Family Herb: Helpful Calendula Blossoms.*

Herbal Academy. https://theherbalacademy.com/a-family-herb-helpful-calendula-blossoms/

Karlsen, K. (n.d.). *Chakra Deities: Keys to Experiencing God in The Hindu Tradition*. Kathleen Karlsen. https://kathleenkarlsen.com/chakras-deities

Kaulja, D. (2022). *Native American Herbalist's Bible*.

Kazan, S. (2022, March 22). *How To Make Hibiscus Tea (Agua De Jamaica | + Mix-Ins)*. Alphafoodie. https://www.alphafoodie.com/how-to-make-hibiscus-tea/#how-to-make-hibiscus-tea

Kristine Marie Corr. (2016). *Chakras : a complete guide to Chakra healing*. Createspace Independent Publishing Platform.

Kronoscode. (2020, February 12). *12 Best Herbal Skincare Products To Add To Your Regimen In 2022*. BHSkin Dermatology. https://bhskin.com/blog/12-best-herbal-skincare-products-2022/

Levis, S. (2019a, January 19). *Plants to Balance the Root Chakra -*. Sow & Dipity. https://www.sowanddipity.com/plants-to-balance-the-root-chakra/

Levis, S. (2019b, January 19). *Plants to Balance the Sacral Chakra -*. Sow & Dipity. https://www.sowanddipity.com/plants-to-balance-the-sacral-chakra/

Levis, S. (2019c, January 19). *Plants to Balance the Solar Plexus Chakra -*. Sow & Dipity. https://www.sowanddipity.com/plants-to-balance-the-solar-plexus-chakra/

Lizzy. (2019, December 5). *Understand The 7 Chakra Colors And What They Mean*. Chakras.info. https://www.chakras.info/chakra-colors/

Lubeck, B. (2021, January 31). *The Health Benefits of Motherwort*. Verywell Health. https://www.verywellhealth.com/the-benefits-of-motherwort-88640

Macfarlane, S. (2021, October 1). *5 Incredible Elderflower Health Benefits*. Wild Dispensary. https://wilddispensary.co.nz/blogs/news/elderflower-health-benefits

Magickal Spot. (2023, March 10). *Mullein: Folklore, Spiritual and Magical Uses*. https://magickalspot.com/mullein/

Marciano, M. (2011, November 18). *Bacopa monnieri*. The Naturopathic Herbalist. https://thenaturopathicherbalist.com/herbs/b-2/bacopa-monnieri/

McDermott, A. (2017, October 10). *Shatavari: Benefits, Side Effects, and*

More. Healthline. https://www.healthline.com/health/food-nutrition/shatavari

McGinley, K. (2020, February 3). 7 Chakra meditations to keep you in balance. Chopra. https://chopra.com/articles/7-chakra-meditations-to-keep-you-in-balance

Medical News Today. (2022, October 10). Astragalus: Benefits, side effects, and frequently asked questions. https://www.medicalnewstoday.com/articles/astragalus-benefits

Mills, T. (2019, October 1). Spiritual Causes of Digestive Problems. Www.youtube.com. https://www.youtube.com/watch?v=wBCFZO5-Ddk

Morgan, A. (2020, August 18). Roots of African American Herbalism: Herbal Use by Enslaved Africans. Herbal Academy. https://theherbalacademy.com/african-american-herbalism-history/

Moules, J. (2019, April 15). Align Your Chakras With These 7 Chakra Yoga Poses. YouAligned^{TM}. https://youaligned.com/chakra-yoga-chakra-alignment/

Mount Sinai Health System. (n.d.). Marshmallow Information | Mount Sinai - New York. Mount Sinai Health System. https://www.mountsinai.org/health-library/herb/marshmallow

Mueller, J. (2020, June 5). The Heart Chakra - Anahata. Solaris Tea. https://solarisbotanicals.com/blogs/lifestyle/the-heart-chakra-anahata

My Ratna. (n.d.). Planets, Chakras and benefits. https://myratna.com/article/planets-chakras-and-benefits

N.D, J. J. (2015, June 9). The Joy of Harvesting and Using Elder Flowers. Herbal Academy. https://theherbalacademy.com/the-joy-of-harvesting-and-using-elder-flowers/

nature of home. (2022, May 25). Growing Ashwagandha Plant: Complete Guide & Essential Tips. https://natureofhome.com/growing-ashwagandha-plant/

Netmeds. (2022, July 3). Shankhpushpi: Benefits, Uses, Dosage, Formulations, and Side Effects. https://www.netmeds.com/health-library/post/shankhpushpi-benefits-uses-dosage-formulations-and-side-effects

O'Bryant, C. (2018, September 3). Sage: The healer, wisdom keeper and spirit releaser... Wild Roots Apothecary. https://www.wildrootsapothe-

cary.com/blogs/herbal-musings/sage-the-healer-wisdom-keeper-and-
spirit-releaser

O'Connor, B. (2015, June 21). 11 Ways to Decalcify Your Pineal Gland
for.... Spirituality+Health. https://www.spiritualityhealth.-
com/blogs/heart-health/2015/06/21/bess-oconnor-how-decalcify-and-
activate-pineal-gland

Ondol Oriental Medicine Clinic. (2022, June 9). Anger, the Wood
Element and the Liver. https://www.ondol.com.au/anger-the-wood-
element-and-the-liver%ef%bf%bc/

Organic India. (2023, January 6). Herbs for the chakras. Organic India.
https://organicindiausa.com/blog/herbs-for-the-chakras/

Pavid, K. (2021, February 19). Aspirin, morphine and chemotherapy: the
essential medicines powered by plants. Natural History Museum.
https://www.nhm.ac.uk/discover/essential-medicines-powered-by-
plants.html

Peppermint Health Benefits. (n.d.). Herbs with Rosalee.
https://www.herbalremediesadvice.org/peppermint-health-benefits.html

Phan, R. (2023a, January 23). What Is Damiana? Verywell Health.
https://www.verywellhealth.com/damiana-what-should-i-know-about-it-
89557

Phan, R. (2023b, March 3). Benefits of the Herb Gotu Kola. Verywell
Health. https://www.verywellhealth.com/the-benefits-of-gotu-kola-89566

Pierce, R. (2021, February 19). How to Grow and Care for Barberry
Bushes | Gardener's Path. Gardener's Path. https://gardenerspath.-
com/plants/ornamentals/grow-barberry/

Planet Ayurveda. (n.d.). Astragalus Root (Astragalus Membranaceus).
Retrieved March 14, 2023, from https://www.planetayurveda.-
com/astragalus-root/

Popham, S. (2015, December 4). Alchemical Herb Profile: Dandelion
(Taraxacum officinale). The School of Evolutionary Herbalism.
https://www.evolutionaryherbalism.com/2015/12/04/alchemical-herb-
profile-dandelion-taraxacum-officinale/

Popham, S. (2016, March 9). How to Connect with Plants and Know
Which Herb is Right for You. Www.youtube.com. https://www.y-
outube.com/watch?v=PrTwSrwHpIY

Preiato, D. (2020, August 6). Capsaicin Supplements: Benefits, Dosage, *and Side Effects. Healthline. https://www.healthline.com/nutri-tion/capsaicin-supplement*

Price, A. (2019, September 11). *This Herb Boosts Heart, Gut & Liver Health ... & May Fight Cancer & Diabetes! Dr. Axe. https://draxe.-com/nutrition/barberry/*

Rasoanaivo, P., Wright, C. W., Willcox, M. L., & Gilbert, B. (2011). *Whole plant extracts versus single compounds for the treatment of malaria: synergy and positive interactions. Malaria Journal, 10(S1). https://doi.org/10.1186/1475-2875-10-s1-s4*

Ricola. (2019a, November 22). *Eucalyptus Shower. https://www.ri-cola.com/en-gb/experience/wellbeing-ideas/article/eucalyptus-shower*

Ricola. (2019b, November 22). *Natural Herbal Steam Bath. https://www.ricola.com/en-gb/experience/wellbeing-ideas/article/natural-herbal-steam-bath*

Rose, K. (2022). *ART & PRACTICE OF SPIRITUAL HERBALISM : transform, heal, and remember with the power of plants and... ancestral medicine. Rockport Publishers.*

Royal Horticultural Society. (n.d.-a). *Chamomile. https://www.rhs.org.uk/herbs/chamomile/grow-your-own*

Royal Horticultural Society. (n.d.-b). *Houseplants: to support human health. https://www.rhs.org.uk/plants/types/houseplants/for-human-health*

Saje US. (n.d.). *The Benefits, Uses, and History of the Peppermint Plant & Peppermint Oil. Retrieved March 11, 2023, from https://www.saje.-com/ingredient-garden-peppermint.html*

Sarah. (2015, November 30). *Sunday Sutra: Sacral Chakra Smoothie. Well and Full. https://wellandfull.com/2015/11/sacral-chakra-smoothie/*

Sarah. (2016a, January 10). *Sunday Sutra: Heart Chakra Smoothie. Well and Full. https://wellandfull.com/2016/01/sunday-sutra-heart-chakra-smoothie/*

Sarah. (2016b, January 31). *Sunday Sutra: Crown Chakra Smoothie. Well and Full. https://wellandfull.com/2016/01/sunday-sutra-crown-chakra-smoothie/*

Sarikaya, A. N. (2019, June 6). *Third Eye Don't Lie tea recipe to unlock your intuition. Mystic Muse. https://mystic-muse.com/third-eye-dont-lie-tea-recipe-to-unlock-your-intuition/*

Sawmill Herb Farm. (n.d.). Elecampane. https://www.sawmillherbfarm.-com/herb%20profile/elecampane/

scienceandnonduality. (2017). Connecting with the Intuitive Guidance of the Heart, Deborah Rozman. In YouTube. https://www.y-outube.com/watch?v=apK8h1B9UbQ

Seaver, V. (n.d.). Health Benefits of Hibiscus Tea, According to a Dietitian. EatingWell. https://www.eatingwell.com/arti-cle/7989695/health-benefits-of-hibiscus-tea-according-to-a-dietitian/

Sencha Tea Bar. (n.d.). How to Make Lavender Tea 4 Different Ways. https://senchateabar.com/blogs/blog/how-to-make-lavender-tea

Sharecare. (n.d.). Who should not use dandelion? | Dandelion. Sharecare. https://www.sharecare.com/health/dandelion/who-should-not-use-dandelion

Shayla, H. (2021, October 28). Benefits and History of Slippery Elm Bark + Tea Recipe. Blog.mountainroseherbs.com. https://blog.mountainrose-herbs.com/slippery-elm-uses-and-benefits

Shrivastava, U. (n.d.). The Seven Chakras of The Human Body and Their Cosmic Connection. Astroyogi. https://www.astroyogi.com/arti-cles/astroyogi-the-seven-chakras-of-the-human-body-and-their-cosmic-connection.aspx

Sierralupe, S. (2020, April 29). Cayenne Pepper - Pocket Herbal. The Practical Herbalist. https://thepracticalherbalist.com/advanced-herbalism/cayenne-pocket-herbal/

Sinadinos, C. (n.d.). Fennel. The Northwest School for Botanical Studies. http://www.herbaleducation.net/fennel

Solidago School of Herbalism. (n.d.). Cinnamon, More Than a Spice! https://www.solidagoherbschool.com

Sow True Seed. (n.d.). Planting Guide and Seed Saving Notes for Mullein. https://sowtrueseed.com/pages/planting-guide-and-seed-saving-notes-for-mullein

StarsandPearls. (2019, May 17). Emotions & Organs: Lungs! Process your Grief! YouTube. https://www.youtube.com/watch?v=l2tVtFjeN9s

Stephan. (2019, December 16). Eyebright - characteristics, cultivation, care and use. Live Native. https://www.live-native.com/eyebright/

Swift, K. (2017, December 17). Fennel: Herb of the Week. CommonWealth Holistic Herbalism. https://commonwealthherb-s.com/fennel-herb-week/

Tharakan, A., Shukla, H., Benny, I. R., Tharakan, M., George, L., & Koshy, S. (2021). Immunomodulatory Effect of Withania somnifera (Ashwagandha) Extract—A Randomized, Double-Blind, Placebo Controlled Trial with an Open Label Extension on Healthy Participants. Journal of Clinical Medicine, 10(16), 3644. https://doi.org/10.3390/jcm10163644

The Daily Struggle. (2022, October 11). Clover: Health Benefits, Magical Properties and Recipes to Try | TDS. https://www.thedailystruggle.co.uk/clover-health-benefits/

The Editors of Encyclopaedia Britannica. (2019). traditional Chinese medicine | Description, History, & Facts. In Encyclopædia Britannica. https://www.britannica.com/science/traditional-Chinese-medicine

The Naturopathic Herbalist. (2011, October 20). Eucalyptus globulus. https://thenaturopathicherbalist.com/herbs/d-f/eucalyptus-globulus/

Thompson, K. (n.d.). Calendula Monograph. HerbRally. https://www.herbrally.com/monographs/calendula

Tiny Rituals. (n.d.). How to Smudge Your Home: A Simple Guide. https://tinyrituals.co/blogs/tiny-rituals/a-simple-guide-to-smudging-your-space

Traditional Medicinals. (n.d.). Peppermint 101. https://www.traditionalmedicinals.com/blogs/ppj/peppermint-101

TruHavn. (n.d.). The Role of the Rose in Herbal Medicine. TruHavn. https://www.truhavn.com/news/the-role-of-rose-in-herbal-medicine

Tryskelion. (2023). Correspondence of Magickal Herbs. https://www.tryskelion.com/mag_correspondence_magickal%20herbs.html

Tyrant Farms. (2020, February 22). How to grow and use milk thistle. https://www.tyrantfarms.com/how-to-grow-and-use-milk-thistle/

Ugaoo. (n.d.). Balance your chakras with these herbs. Ugaoo. https://www.ugaoo.com/blogs/green-lifestyle/how-to-balance-chakras-with-chakra-herbs

US Forest Service. (n.d.). Medicinal Botany. Www.fs.usda.gov. https://www.fs.usda.gov/wildflowers/ethnobotany/medicinal/index.shtml

Van Fossen, A. (2019, July 23). How to Align Your Energy with the Four Phases of the Moon. https://allievanfossen.com/how-to-align-your-energy-with-the-four-phases-of-the-moon/

Veeresham, C. (2012). Natural products derived from plants as a source of drugs. Journal of Advanced Pharmaceutical Technology & Research,

3(4), 200. https://doi.org/10.4103/2231-4040.104709

Vidaurri, E. (2016, January 10). Elderberry Herbal Tea. Recipes to Nourish. https://www.recipestonourish.com/elderberry-herbal-tea/

Washington College. (n.d.). Ashwaganda - Withania somnifera. https://www.washcoll.edu/learn-by-doing/food/plants/solanaceae/withania-somnifera.php

Wattanathorn, J., Mator, L., Muchimapura, S., Tongun, T., Pasuriwong, O., Piyawatkul, N., Yimtae, K., Sripanidkulchai, B., & Singkhoraard, J. (2008). Positive modulation of cognition and mood in the healthy elderly volunteer following the administration of Centella asiatica. Journal of Ethnopharmacology, 116(2), 325–332. https://doi.org/10.1016/j.jep.2007.11.038

Web MD. (n.d.). ELDERFLOWER: Overview, Uses, Side Effects, Precautions, Interactions, Dosing and Reviews. https://www.webmd.com/vitamins/ai/ingredientmono-708/elderflower

WebMDWe. (2010). Inulin: Uses, Side Effects, Interactions, Dosage, and Warning. Web MD. https://www.webmd.com/vitamins/ai/ingredientmono-1048/inulin

Weiss, J. (2015, September 4). Lung Healing Sound to release grief, sadness and disappointment. Www.youtube.com. https://www.youtube.com/watch?v=3JV4ACtvxxM

White, A. (2017, July 10). Are Phytoestrogens Good for You? Healthline. https://www.healthline.com/health/phytoestrogens

Williams, J. (2022a). What is Spiritual Herbalism? https://www.youtube.com/watch?v=RyiHA2UQn5g

Williams, J. (2022b). Spiritual Herbalism. Aeon Books.

Witchy Gypsy Momma. (2021a, January 6). Magickal and Medicinal Herbs: Sage 101. Witchy Gypsy Momma. https://witchygypsymomma.com/2021/01/06/digging-deeper-into-sage/

Witchy Gypsy Momma. (2021b, January 20). Magickal and Medicinal Herbs: Eucalyptus 101. https://witchygypsymomma.com/2021/01/20/digging-deeper-into-eucalyptus/

Wszelaki, M. (2016, April 1). Chasteberry Tea to Alleviate PMS and Menopause Symptoms. Hormones & Balance. https://hormonesbalance.com/recipes/chasteberry-tea-pms-menopause/

Wszelaki, M. (2020a, January 22). Milk Thistle Ginger Tea for Liver Health. Hormones & Balance. https://hormonesbalance.-

com/recipes/milk-thistle-ginger-tea-for-liver-health/

Wszelaki, M. (2020b, March 11). Soothing Calendula Lotion for Dry, Irritated Skin. Hormones & Balance. https://hormonesbalance.-com/recipes/calendula-lotion-for-dry-irritated-skin/

Wszelaki, M. (2020c, October 8). Herbal Honey Recipe to Protect Against Colds & Flu—Rosemary, Sage, Thyme. Hormones and Balance. https://hormonesbalance.com/recipes/herbal-honey-for-hormones-and-immunity/

Zak, V. (2009). 20,000 Secrets of Tea. Random House Publishing Group.

YOUR FEEDBACK IS VALUED

We would like to be so bold as to ask for an act of kindness from you. If you read and enjoyed our book/s, would you please consider leaving an honest review on Amazon or audible? As an independent publishing group, your feedback means the absolute world to us. We read every single review we receive and would love to hear your thoughts, as each piece of feedback helps us serve you better. Your feedback may also impact others across the globe, helping them discover powerful knowledge they can implement in their lives to give them hope and self-empowerment. Wishing you empowerment, courage, and wisdom on your journey.

If you have read or listened to any of our books and would be so kind as to review them, you can do so by clicking the 'learn more' tab under the book's picture on our website:

https://ascendingvibrations.net/books

Why not join our Facebook community and discuss your spiritual path with like-minded seekers?

We would love to hear from you!

Go here to join the 'Ascending Vibrations' community:

bit.ly/ascendingvibrations